introducing **orchids**

introducing **orchids**

WILMA AND
BRIAN RITTERSHAUSEN

PHOTOGRAPHY BY LINDA BURGESS

Trafalgar Square Publishing

First published in the United States of America in 2002 by
Trafalgar Square Publishing
North Pomfret, Vermont 05053

Printed and bound in Singapore

Editorial Director: Jane O'Shea
Creative Director: Mary Evans
Design Assistant: Katy Davis
Project Editor: Hilary Mandleberg
Production: Tracy Hart

ISBN 1-57076-229-5

Library of Congress Catalog Card Number:
2002104273

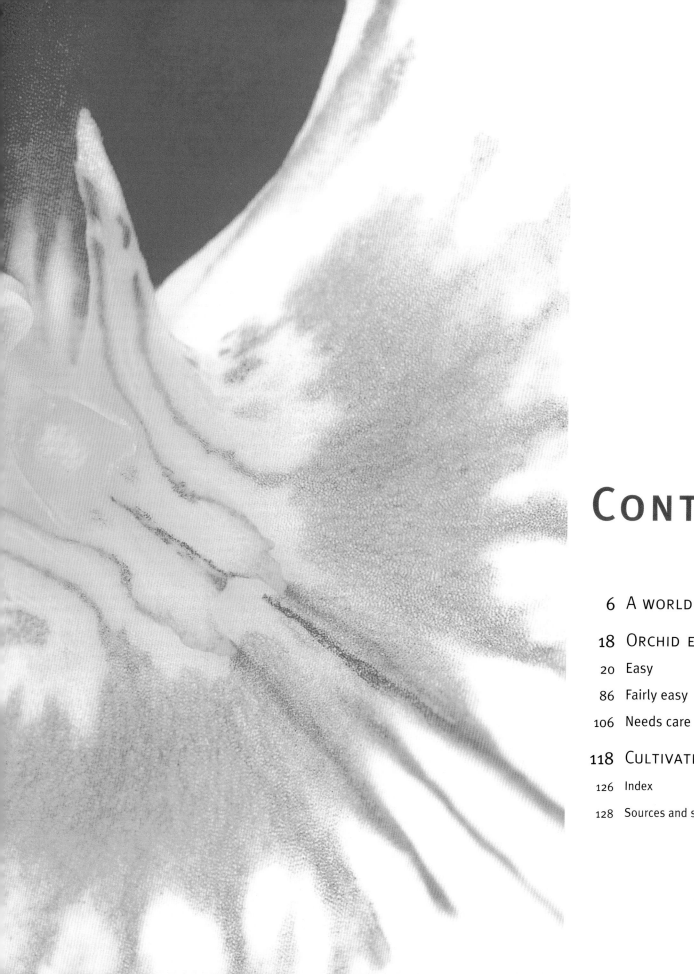

Contents

A WORLD OF ORCHIDS

Very often one's first encounter with orchids is an eye-catching display of flowering sprays in a store window. But to see orchids at their best at an orchid show is a breathtaking experience. So varied are the multitude of blooms— which, at first glance, can be difficult to recognize as belonging to the same family—that you cannot help but be left with a desire to know more. These are the "hobby orchids," grown by enthusiasts the world over and loved for their mystery and elegance combined with ease of growing, quite unimaginable in other plants.

As with all flowering plants, the classification of orchids is based on the structure of the blooms. Orchids are, in the main, insect pollinated and despite their diversity, each conforms to one basic pattern. Until you have become more familiar with its many variations, this pattern may be hard to recognize. The flower consists of three sepals that form the outside of the closed bud. As the bud opens, three inner petals are revealed. The third petal is different from the other two, and is distinguished by its shape and colorings. It has developed into a lip, or labellum, which serves as a landing stage for the pollinator. At the center of the flower is the column, a finger-like structure that carries the pollen.

Uniquely, the millions of pollen grains are compressed into small, solid packages for an insect to carry from one flower to the next. The seed capsules can contain anything up to a million tiny seeds. In nature, these need the assistance of a microscopic mycorrhizal fungus before they will germinate, and only a very few will be successful. In cultivation, the seed is sown on a prepared medium in sterile jars containing the nutrients and trace elements required to replace the natural mycorrhiza. In this way, it is possible to germinate 100 percent of the seeds, so the number that can be raised is almost limitless. Over many years, this has led to a huge proliferation of hybrids. Orchids are slow growing and, depending upon the genus, can take up to five years or longer to flower. However, they are extremely long lived, and once a well-cultivated plant reaches maturity, it will continue to grow and bloom for many years.

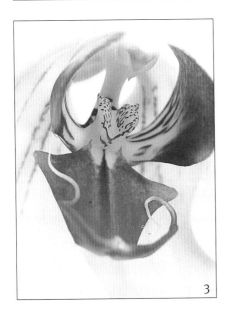

A DIVERSITY OF SPECIES

Species orchids are the naturally occurring, wild plants, and there are estimated to be between 25,000 and 30,000 different types spread throughout the world. Whichever figure is accepted, it is a formidable total of plants that places orchids up among the largest families of flowering plants.

Terrestrial orchids

Orchids grow in almost every natural environment. In northern Canada and Siberia, where long, severe winters are followed by short summers, small terrestrial (soil-growing) orchids like cypripediums (ladies' slipper orchids)—which are also found throughout Europe—develop and bloom in just a few weeks during the summer snow melt, before dying down again for the winter. Most terrestrial orchids—which include the European genera *Dactylorhiza* (marsh and spotted orchids) and *Orchis*—produce underground tubers and a single stem with leaves that extends into the flowering spike and is renewed annually.

Terrestrial orchids occur over many of the world's land masses, and in grasslands and woodlands in parts of Europe where agriculture is less intensive, they often grow in profusion. Elsewhere, they are found in habitats ranging from dry Australian deserts, which have their own unique orchid flora, to high mountain plateaux.

Epiphytes and lithophytes

However, the cultivated orchids that excite the greatest interest are the epiphytes. These are "air plants," which occur mostly in the tropical and subtropical rain forests and areas close to the equator. Although they literally grow on trees, these orchids are not parasites: like bromeliads, they use the trees simply to gain a position that enjoys better light and air. Epiphytes such as vandas, which have long, freely suspended aerial roots, can exist only where temperatures are sufficiently high to prevent their exposed aerial roots from freezing.

Many epiphytic orchids, like the odontoglossums and miltoniopsis (pansy orchids) whose natural home is in the Andes mountain range of South America, grow at high altitudes. Here they can be found at up to 6,500 feet (2,000 meters), where the air is crisp and cool and the nights often frosty. In cultivation, such exposure would greatly damage the plants, but in the rarefied air at high altitudes they come to no harm. The orchids produce their growth during the monsoons, and it is completed as the dry

season approaches. Then the plants rest, or become dormant, a state that may last for anything from a few weeks to several months. Some, like the lycastes from Central America, will lose part or all of their foliage, flowering and making new growth—which they do simultaneously—only when the rains start up again.

The tropical and subtropical orchids that are the subject of this book are mostly modern hybrids mainly derived from epiphytes growing in the wild in the tropical rain forests. Many of these epiphytes have evolved over thousands of years, experiencing little disturbance in an unchanging environment. In a rain forest, one large, mature tree carrying a multitude of orchids can be likened to an apartment block in which every floor up to roof level is occupied. In an Asian rain forest, where the tree first forks, the trunk will hold large clumps of orchids such as cymbidiums and coelogynes, while in Central and South America there will be cattleyas and laelias. Toward the higher, thinner branches are smaller species, which may include odontoglossums, oncidiums, and masdevallias in South America, and bulbophyllums in Southeast Asia. The "penthouse" or canopy of the tree will be occupied by the smallest "twig" epiphytes, tiny miniatures too numerous to name, living life on the edge. All these orchids will receive varying amounts of dappled sunlight and shade from the trees, and moisture from the mists and rains that sweep in during the monsoon season.

Some orchids also grow on rock faces, and these are called lithophytes. They include the paphiopedilums (slipper orchids) and, perhaps best known of this type, the phragmipediums. Since in nature the lithophytes obtain their nutrients in a similar way to the epiphytes, their culture is the same. In each case, nutrients are washed down the surface of the tree bark, or down the rock face, to be absorbed by the orchids' firmly clinging roots. While some roots remain exposed, others grow into any cracks and crevices and feed on the natural mycelium (fungal spawn) that exists there. Oncidiums, in particular, often produce dense mats of fine roots for this purpose.

1. *Dendrobium* Siam Jewel
2. *Masdevallia* Marguerite
3. *Phalaenopsis* Happy Girl
4. *Paphiopedilum* Maudiae
5. *Cymbidium* Tracey's Hill
6. *Miltoniopsis* Red Tide

Cymbidiums are typical sympodial orchids with pseudobulbs. These are swollen stems designed for water retention that provide moisture for the plant during periods of drought in their country of origin. Note the new growths which, as they develop into pseudobulbs, will produce the next flower spikes.

Sympodial orchids

The majority of epiphytic and lithophytic orchids are sympodial, meaning that they produce either new pseudobulbs or leafy growths each season.

Orchids that produce pseudobulbs include cymbidiums, coelogynes, and bulbophyllums from Asia, cattleyas, odontoglossums, miltoniopsis, and laelias from Central and South America, and dendrobiums from Asia and Australia. A pseudobulb is similar to an iris tuber and, despite the name, quite unlike a true bulb, such as a narcissus. It consists of a swollen stem that stores moisture to support the plant during its dormant period. A new pseudobulb develops each year from the base of the previous one, until a series is built up. Each pseudobulb will be larger than the previous one, until the maximum size is achieved. Eventually, old pseudobulbs die, leaving the newer ones to perpetuate the plant. In this way, the orchids can live for many years—in the wild, their lifespan is often determined by that of the trees upon which they grow.

Pseudobulbs vary in size and shape, from plump like a hen's egg in the odontoglossums, miltoniopsis, and coelogynes, to long and thin like a bamboo

Dendrobiums are sympodial orchids, with long, slender "canes" that serve the same function as pseudobulbs. Many dendrobiums shed their leaves in fall and remain semidormant in winter.

Paphiopedilums are sympodial orchids that do not produce pseudobulbs. In their place are fleshy growths. Note the new growth emerging from the base of the previously matured growths.

cane in the widespread and varied dendrobiums. They may grow to 3 feet (1 meter) long, as in *Dendrobium pierardii*, or be as small as a fingernail, as in some bulbophyllums. The longer ones, such as certain dendrobiums, grow downward, while others, like the cattleyas and laelias, remain rigidly upright. The aerial roots, which in cultivation may grow in the pot, support the pseudobulbs, which in turn support the leaves. These vary in number and may be annual or live for several years before dying, leaving the pseudobulb bare for the remainder of its life.

The paphiopedilums from Asia and phragmipediums from Central and South America are examples of sympodial orchids that do not have pseudobulbs. Instead, they produce leafy growths consisting of fleshy foliage that retains the moisture reserves for the plant.

Sympodial orchids produce their blooms on flower spikes, which usually come from the newest growth as in cymbidiums, odontoglossums, and brassias. The spikes may be long or short and arise from the base of the pseudobulb, as in cymbidiums, or from the top, as in cattleyas and encyclias. Alternatively, they may grow from the center of the new growth before the pseudobulb has matured, in the manner of some coelogynes and rossioglossums. Discovering how each plant produces its blooms is yet another fascinating aspect of growing orchids.

Monopodial orchids

Phalaenopsis (moth orchids), vandas, ascocentrums, and aerides, which come from the Far East and the Philippines, are all examples of monopodial orchids. This means that they grow from single or multiple stems, from the tip of which new leaves are produced to form a fan-like growth with foliage extending on alternate sides of the stem. These plants can be very short and compact, like the phalaenopsis, or may grow into tall, sometimes straggly specimens like the vandas and related plants. Their flower spikes appear from the leaf axils at the side of the main stem, which does not interfere with the progress of growth. From the bare stem at the base of the plant, fleshy white roots—silvery and flattened in phalaenopsis— will grow, and will adhere to any surface with which they come into contact.

A WEALTH OF HYBRIDS

Over a century and a half of orchid hybridizing has led to a huge proliferation of new varieties. Long breeding lines have emerged that have resulted in new colors, shapes, and sizes of blooms, creating even more variation than is found among the species. Today, new varieties or grexes are registered with the Royal Horticultural Society in Great Britain, which is the world authority for the registration of orchid hybrids. The number of registered hybrids currently stands at over 100,000, a figure that is increasing by 3,000 each year and testifies to the extraordinary breeding properties of orchids.

However, only the very best of these hybrids are used for commercial production. Hybrid genera such as *Vuylstekeara*, which is a combination of three natural genera (*Cochlioda* x *Miltonia* x *Odontoglossum*), are more vigorous and often more tolerant of temperature variations than are the species. Consequently, they are in greater demand and are far more suitable for a beginner to grow. In fact, many species orchids are now very rare in the wild.

Orchids like this highly decorative modern Odontoglossum-type hybrid will produce their exquisite blooms on sprays called flower spikes approximately every nine to twelve months. The flower spikes come from the base of the newly matured pseudobulb and may grow to 1½ feet (45cm) or more with, in some hybrids, up to fifty blooms. These will often last for five to six weeks in perfection. The taller flower spikes will need to be supported by bamboo canes as they grow. When the flowers have finished, cut the flower spike down to the base.

THE NAMING OF ORCHIDS

The orchid family is divided into genera (singular "genus") and the first part of the orchid's name, written in italics, is that of the genus, for example *Cymbidium*. There are naturally occurring genera such as *Odontoglossum* and *Cymbidium*, and artificial genera that can be a combination of two or more, for example: *Odontoglossum* x *Cochlioda* = *Odontioda* *Cattleya* x *Laelia* = *Laeliocattleya*.

The name following the genus is that of the grex, which may be species or hybrid. If a species, it is written in italics, for example *Cymbidium lowianum*; if a hybrid it is written in roman type, as in *Cymbidium* Cherry Blossom.

The third name can belong to the individual clone or plant, and not to all plants from the same species or hybrid, in which case it appears in single quotation marks, for example *Dendrobium* Stardust 'Chyomi,' or it may be a botanically recognized variety as in *Cymbidium lowianum* var. *concolor*.

Seed-raised plants of the same grex can vary in color because seedlings from one cross will all be individual, hence they also have a third, varietal, name to distinguish them, for example *Cymbidium* Cherry Blossom 'Perfection.' Mass-produced plants will all be identical, as in *Vuylstekeara* Cambria 'Plush.'

Hybridizing among the zygopetalums (above) and allied – closely related – orchids has been growing significantly in recent years, with huge advances being made in Australia, where there appears to be no limit to the wonderful and varied hybrids being raised.

ORCHIDS TO GROW

It is possible to grow orchids from many parts of the world in one place under the same conditions. For example, in tropical gardens, where tropical conditions are recreated, you will see orchids from as far apart as East Africa and Indonesia growing with others from the Himalayas and Andes mountain ranges.

A widespread hobby

In the relatively mild climate of Western Europe, temperatures are never too extreme. Here, it is possible to grow most tropical orchids in the controlled environment of a greenhouse or conservatory. This is a tradition that started in Britain during the Victorian era and soon spread to other countries in Europe. Originally, large ornate conservatories were constructed to house huge collections of the finest tropical orchids, which at that time were taken straight from the newly explored tropical forests of Southeast Asia, Central and South America, and East Africa in particular.

Today, throughout Western Europe, the fashion has shifted from greenhouse culture to growing mainly a few modern hybrids—mostly cymbidiums, odontoglossums, miltoniopsis, phalaenopsis, and paphiopedilums—often on windowsills

Phragmipediums (above) are known as 'slipper orchids,' a name which refers to the pouch that adorns the bloom. The pouch is a further modification of the lip and serves the same purpose, temporarily trapping, but not injuring, the pollinating insect.

Lip markings on cymbidiums (opposite) are varied and can be colorful or plain, often forming the most spectacular part of the bloom. The original purpose of these markings was to attract pollinating insects to the right place so they could pollinate the flower.

in the home. However, what starts with two or three manageable plants can, within a few years, all too easily escalate into a totally absorbing and ever-expanding hobby. A greenhouse or conservatory then becomes a necessity rather than a luxury.

The North American scene

In North America, climatic conditions are many and varied. The most inhospitable regions for orchids are the desert States in the United States, where conditions are extremely hot and dry. Greenhouses or shade-cloth houses cannot be kept cool or moist enough for any but the hardiest of orchids, while indoors the constant air conditioning needed to reduce the temperature creates a very dry atmosphere, which again is unsuitable for orchids—humidity can only be kept up in an enclosed indoor growing case, for example.

By contrast, in Florida the hot, humid weather that prevails for most of the year enables tropical orchids from around the globe to be grown outdoors, and cattleyas, laelias, vandas, phalaenopsis, oncidiums, dendrobiums, encyclias, and others may be established on trees. The real challenge here lies in growing the high-altitude orchids like the odontoglossums and miltoniopsis, which are so easy in cooler areas.

The coastal areas from California to Vancouver have proved more suitable for growing cool-climate orchids outdoors, and here cymbidiums, zygopetalums, phragmipediums, and paphiopedilums thrive. Only where the night temperature drops to below 50°F (10°C) do the orchids need to be brought inside.

In some parts of Canada, where permafrost penetrates the ground, conventional greenhouses cannot be maintained, so instead enthusiasts grow orchids in their large basements where the house's furnace is located. The orchids are placed on a slatted bench above staging, as they would be in a conventional greenhouse (see page 122), while artificial lighting is supplied on a time switch to mimic day and night. Under these conditions, it is mostly the smaller-growing, compact orchids such as odontoglossums, brassias, masdevallias, encyclias, and paphiopedilums that do well. In summer they benefit from a short respite outdoors in the shade.

BUYING ORCHIDS

Rossioglossum *Rawdon Jester (above) is known as the 'clown orchid' for the small, colorful, man-like structure at the base of the lip. This is a further adaptation of the "honey guide," although no nectar is produced by this flower.*

Phalaenopsis (opposite) have small, neat lips which can be colored or plain. There is a comparatively small landing area for the pollinating insect, which can be guided in by the wide, often delicately patterned sepals and petals.

The opportunities for obtaining orchid plants are today far greater than ever before. In many parts of the world they can be found on sale in garden centers, flower shops, and even in supermarkets, where some of the most saleable varieties are usually stocked. In outlets such as these the plants displayed are in full flower and little cultural information is given other than a label with brief instructions to "water once a week and keep in shade." Often, the plants are in decorative containers to enhance their saleability. Unlike flowerpots, however, such containers have no holes in the base and, without the all-important drainage, when overwatered, the roots can quickly rot. Plants are also sometimes adorned with ribbons, or twisted willow sticks, and their foliage sprayed with artificial glitter. Clearly these plants are not for the serious grower!

What has happened is that the big commercial nurseries have created a "disposal market" and these orchids are bred to satisfy that need. They are produced in their millions, for a short life, in exactly the same way as poinsettias and Christmas trees. How many of them survive for another year? Although they can be grown on, few people will wait months for the orchid to bloom again, and so it is replaced with another one

that is in flower. If fresh, orchid blooms will last for several months, so even in this "disposal" form they represent better value than a flower arrangement of cut blooms that will be past its best within a week or two, but will cost the same to buy.

Moving on

Once successfully started with these "disposal orchids," you may find yourself encouraged to take care of your plants for longer—if so, the time has come to visit an orchid nursery or a major exhibition. This will open up a whole new world of varied and beautiful orchids, and provide an opportunity for you to find out more about the plants. Additional orchids on sale will include everything from exciting new seedlings offering the promise of fulfilling a dream, to super-size plants just budding or in fresh bloom, and from the rarest and most unusual orchids in cultivation to the more popular beginners' types. Professional growers will gladly give cultural advice and sell a range of books, step-by-step videos, and sundries such as fertilizers and potting mixes.

If you cannot get to a nursery or exhibition, some orchid nurseries offer a mail-order service. Most produce a catalog or price list and have their own

Web site for on-line ordering. In addition, there may also be an orchid society somewhere near you, where new members are always welcome and where you will learn a lot about the plants from other enthusiasts.

Importing orchids

When your hobby has progressed as far as looking for rarities, be wary of importing orchids from another country. You will need to check your own and the exporting country's plant health regulations. Within the European Union there is free movement of plants without any restriction, but elsewhere—for example, between Britain and the United States—permits are required. The onus is on the importer to abide by their own country's ruling, not on the exporter to check what is allowed.

Australia, being an island continent, is the most difficult place into which to import plants of any sort; a long period of quarantine is strictly enforced, and the losses that can occur as a result of this make importing orchids uneconomical for Australian citizens. To avoid the disappointment of having the orchids you purchased while on holiday confiscated when you return home, make sure you have obtained all the necessary documents beforehand. In other words, it is always easier to buy from a local supplier!

ORCHID EXTRAVAGANZA

Orchids need different temperature ranges, which are determined by their country of origin and the altitude at which they grow naturally. High-altitude plants from South America, such as odontoglossums, need to be grown in cooler conditions than, say, phalaenopsis from the Philippines, which are seldom found above 3,000 feet (1,000 meters) and need warmer conditions. The popular cymbidiums can be grown in the same temperature range as odontoglossums but need more light. This is why they can be placed outdoors in summer in most places.

Depending on which part of the world you live in, it may be possible to grow all the orchids mentioned here, plus many more. If you cannot provide any extra warmth, you can build up a collection entirely with cool-growing orchids. On the other hand, in an average indoor environment, you can "mix and match" by finding cooler and warmer areas within your home.

Just remember that these orchids will not, however, all grow alongside each other. The major orchid-growing regions of the world are located in areas where the climate is less extreme, or can be modified under controlled conditions. As we have seen, one of the hardest climates to manipulate is one that is hot and dry: it is extremely difficult to lower the temperature while at the same time increasing and maintaining humidity. So what can be described as an "easy" orchid in some parts of the world may not necessarily be so in others.

We have attempted to address the problem by dividing this book into three sections—"easy," "fairly easy," and "needs care." Each of these is defined, and cultivation advice within each section of the book is only given if an orchid requires some more specific care.

EASY

We define "easy" orchids as those that can be grown indoors in mild climates in homes that have the heating on during the daytime in winter.

Some of the most exciting and rewarding orchids are contained in this section, and there is no lack of variety. In addition to those described there are many more, as can be discovered by visiting an orchid nursery or an orchid exhibition. The orchids mentioned here vary enormously in size, which is why we give the approximate height of an average adult plant and the size of pot you may expect it to be growing in at the time of purchase.

You may decide to start with the most conveniently sized plants, which will fit neatly on a windowsill or plant trolley. These include the delicately patterned *Odontoglossum* types, which on their own can provide an exciting mix of colors and shapes. Some of the orchids described are very much smaller and can be enchanting to grow in a small, enclosed container such as a disused fish tank.

At the other end of the scale are the cymbidiums—big, colorful, and delightful, but space-demanding plants that are best in a sun lounge or conservatory where they can be fully appreciated and enjoyed. Wherever you intend to grow your orchids, the choice is a wide one!

CYMBIDIUM SUE

This beautiful summer-flowering hybrid was bred in 1980 and is well worth seeking out. Free-flowering, its vibrant apple-green blooms will last for two months but do not all open at the same time: as the flowers on the first spike are about to open, other spikes will be less advanced, ensuring a long flowering season. The plant will make several new growths in one season and can easily be grown on to make a large specimen within a few years. Alternatively, it can be divided to maintain it at a specific size.

FLOWER SIZE: 3 INCHES (8CM) ACROSS
FLOWER SPIKE: 2¹/₂ FEET (75CM)
PLANT HEIGHT: 25 INCHES (63CM)
POT SIZE: 8 INCHES (20CM)

CYMBIDIUM TRACEY'S HILL

Not a true miniature, this is a compact hybrid that remains smaller than the standard types. A fine modern variety from 1995, young plants produce several flower spikes, each bearing up to a dozen blooms. These appear in the fall and can last as long as eight weeks; the color is a deep, non-fading yellow with a red stripe down the center of the sepals and petals. While not a plant to be grown in the tropics, in temperate areas it ranks high among the easy favorites for indoor or cool greenhouse culture.

FLOWER SIZE: 2³/₄IN (7CM) ACROSS
FLOWER SPIKE: 16 INCHES (40CM)
PLANT HEIGHT: 26 INCHES (65CM)
POT SIZE: 8 INCHES (20CM)

CYMBIDIUM SLEEPING GIANT

This Australian-bred hybrid from 1974 comes from a line of "Sleeping" hybrids, its parents being *C.* Sleeping Beauty and *C.* Sleeping Monarch. It is a standard *Cymbidium*, needing space to spread and sufficient headroom for its tall flower spikes. The plant is large and robust, with rounded pseudobulbs and several long leaves. The flower spikes appear toward the end of the summer growing season, when the pseudobulbs are maturing. The spikes grow steadily over the winter to bloom in early spring, when the flowers will last for eight weeks or more. Each flower spike can be expected to carry eight to ten gorgeous ivory-white blooms.

FLOWER SIZE: 4½ INCHES (11CM) ACROSS
FLOWER SPIKE: 40 INCHES (1M)
PLANT HEIGHT: 2 FEET (60CM)
POT SIZE: 10 INCHES (25CM)

CYMBIDIUM BEAUPORT

This hybrid, raised in 1995 in Jersey in the Channel Islands, is one of a multitude of modern hybrids that exhibit the vibrant colors associated with this type of breeding, and that have come a long way from the original species. Among cymbidiums, every color—with the exception of the elusive blue—can be found. This plant needs space to grow well and, as with all cymbidiums, it can be placed outdoors for the summer growing season in a position sheltered from the midday sun and the worst of the wind and rain. Bring the plant indoors, to its cool winter quarters, well before the first frosts are expected, by which time it should be showing the new season's flower spikes. Do not move the plant while it is in advanced bud, or the buds may drop off. It will reward you with ten to twelve blooms to a flower spike.

FLOWER SIZE: 4 INCHES (10CM) ACROSS
FLOWER SPIKE: 40 INCHES (1M)
PLANT HEIGHT: 2 FEET (60CM)
POT SIZE: 10 INCHES (25CM)

CYMBIDIUM RED BAKER

This is an attractive, early-season hybrid that produces upright flower spikes with up to a dozen blooms during the fall. The flower spikes last well into winter. It is one among many hundreds of compact types raised around the world during the last twenty years for the pot-plant trade. However, it is not difficult to keep this hybrid going year after year with the minimum of attention indoors, or in a cool greenhouse. Placing it outdoors for the summer will greatly increase its flowering capacity the following year.

FLOWER SIZE: 2¹/₂ INCHES (6CM) ACROSS
FLOWER SPIKE: 16 INCHES (40CM)
PLANT HEIGHT: 26 INCHES (65CM)
POT SIZE: 8 INCHES (20CM)

CYMBIDIUM CHERRY BLOSSOM 'PERFECTION'

This is a true miniature, which produces numerous flowers lasting up to five weeks on drooping flower spikes during the fall. It is a primary hybrid between C. erythrostylum from Vietnam and C. floribundum (syn. C. pumilum) from Japan. Bred in the United States in 1963, 'Perfection' adds a valuable dimension to the variety of midwinter flowering clones. The plant is compact with small, rounded pseudobulbs and short leaves. The unique shape of the forward-thrusting petals are a trait derived from C. erythrostylum.

FLOWER SIZE: 2 INCHES (5CM) ACROSS
FLOWER SPIKE: 1 FOOT (30CM)
PLANT HEIGHT: 1 FOOT (30CM)
POT SIZE: 6 INCHES (15CM)

CYMBIDIUM SUMMER PEARL 'SHIRLEY'

Extensive breeding with selected species has given rise to a wonderful range of summer-flowering cymbidiums, unknown half a century ago, extending the season to almost the whole year. Among these recently introduced varieties white is a much sought-after color, and this delightful clone of *C*. Summer Pearl, introduced in 1984, has the right qualities, plus a combination of white sepals and petals with a deeply margined red lip, which make it one of the top varieties. The plant is compact, and this, together with the freedom with which it blooms—it produces a dozen or more flowers that last six to eight weeks—makes it a suitable candidate for growing as a houseplant.

FLOWER SIZE: 3 INCHES (8CM) ACROSS
FLOWER SPIKE: 2¹/₂ FEET (75CM)
PLANT HEIGHT: 25 INCHES (63CM)
POT SIZE: 8 INCHES (20CM)

Coelogyne flaccida

This is an exquisite species, introduced from the east Himalayas and described by John Lindley in 1830. It has cone-shaped pseudobulbs each with a pair of hard, stiffly held green leaves. The pendent flower spikes emerge from the base of the mature pseudobulbs in early spring. The flowers—up to six or eight per spike—are a pale buff-cream with delicate lip markings in yellow. They are strongly fragrant and will last for two to three weeks in perfection. This is an easy plant to grow provided it is given a rest in cool conditions in winter while it remains dormant.

FLOWER SIZE: 1^1/$_2$ INCHES (4CM) ACROSS
FLOWER SPIKE: 8 INCHES (20CM)
PLANT HEIGHT: 10 INCHES (25CM)
POT SIZE: 3 INCHES (8CM)

DENDROBIUM NOBILE VAR. *ALBIFLORUM*

This species was introduced into cultivation in 1830 from its native home—which stretches from South China across India to Thailand—where it grows on trees as an epiphyte. Under these conditions it receives plenty of rain during the monsoon season, followed by a period of drought during which the plant becomes dormant. In cultivation it grows best in a cool position, with full light during the winter. This will initiate the flower buds, which form along the mature canes in early spring. This plant is a highly collectable semi-alba form of *D. nobile*. It lacks the light mauve-pink coloring of the type, and is one of a number of recognized color forms from a species that has contributed a great deal to the modern hybrids that now abound.

FLOWER SIZE: 3 INCHES (8CM) ACROSS
FLOWER SPIKE: NONE
PLANT HEIGHT: 1½ FEET (45CM)
POT SIZE: 4 INCHES (10CM)

Laeliocattleya Quo Vadis 'Floralia'

Here we have one of the largest and most flamboyant of the *Cattleya* hybrids. It was raised in France in 1948. Its gorgeously rich coloring has an almost translucent quality and the plant is typical of many similar hybrids that were at the peak of their favor around the 1950's. With their large pseudobulbs and tough leaves, these plants can be quite demanding of space. They should be kept on the dry side during winter after flowering and while not in growth. 'Floralia' is the result of long breeding lines, the majority of which produce the rich mauves and purples for which this genus is renowned. The flowers, borne on short spikes, appear at various times during the summer and fall and will last for up to six weeks.

Flower size: 7 inches (18cm) across
Plant height: 1¹/₂ feet (45cm)
Pot size: 7 inches (18cm)

Cattleya intermedia x *Brassolaeliocattleya* Chinese Jade

This new and as yet unnamed hybrid has the classic shape of flared sepals nicely balanced by the proportions of the lip and the coloring so often sought among this type. The large, fragrant blooms appear during the summer and fall months, with one or two arising on a short spike from the newly completed pseudobulb. The blooms will last for up to three weeks. Combining three genera— *Brassavola, Laelia,* and *Cattleya*— this hybrid performs best in intermediate temperatures and good light. Rest the plant by keeping it dry when not in active growth.

FLOWER SIZE: 5 INCHES (12CM) ACROSS
PLANT HEIGHT: 1 FOOT (30CM)
POT SIZE: 6 INCHES (15CM)

CATTLEYA BRAZILIENSIS

This is an example of a hybrid that occurs naturally in the wild. It was discovered when the cross of C. bicolor and C. harrisoniana was made artificially and the resulting seedlings were identical to C. braziliensis. The plant comes from the rain forests of Brazil, which is home to many members of this lovely genus. The flowers are similar in shape and color to those of C. harrisoniana, while C. bicolor gives the plant a robust quality. Both parents and hybrid are bifoliate, meaning that their slender pseudobulbs each support two broadly oval leaves. The flowers, with several to a spike, emerge from between the leaves when the pseudobulb has matured. Slightly fragrant, they appear in summer and will last for about three weeks.

FLOWER SIZE: 3 INCHES (8CM) ACROSS
FLOWER SPIKE: 3 INCHES (8CM)
PLANT HEIGHT: 20 INCHES (50CM)
POT SIZE: 7 INCHES (18CM)

CATTLEYA BOB ELLIOTT

This delightful, fragrant cattleya is very similar to the species *C. mossiae*, which is one of its parents. The similarities lie in the open shape of the flower and the coloring on the lip. Usually just a single bloom is produced on a short spike from the apex of the long pseudobulb. This bloom can last up to three weeks. Its pale lilac coloring is bordering on the elusive blue, which is a constant challenge for the breeders of these fine orchids. This is a British hybrid, raised in 1993 in a range that as yet is quite restricted. It flowers in spring and summer, and requires intermediate temperatures and good light.

FLOWER SIZE: 5$^1/_2$ INCHES (14CM) ACROSS
PLANT HEIGHT: 16 INCHES (40CM)
POT SIZE: 6 INCHES (15CM)

SOPHROLAELIOCATTLEYA MADGE FORDYCE 'RED ORB'

This compact-growing dazzler takes its name from the three separate genera that produced it in 1971 in the United States: *Sophronitis* provides the brilliant color and small pseudobulbs, with *Laelia* and *Cattleya* contributing to the hybrid vigor. The plant soon becomes multi-leaded, enabling it to be grown into a specimen producing a mass of single blooms lasting three to four weeks on short flower spikes during the summer. It needs cool to intermediate temperatures and will do well on a light windowsill, but it must be kept fairly dry while flowering.

FLOWER SIZE: 2 INCHES (5CM) ACROSS
PLANT HEIGHT: 10 INCHES (25CM)
POT SIZE: 3–4 INCHES (8–10CM)

BRASSOLAELIOCATTLEYA CHEF D'OEUVRE 'ETOLLE'

This unusual and brightly colored hybrid was raised in France in 1986. The olive-green petals and sepals make a striking contrast to the ruby-red lip. A specific breeding line has given rise to the open shape of the flower, which carries a hint of fragrance handed down from the *Cattleya* side. The slender pseudobulbs are quite tall, producing one to two flowers from the apex when fully mature. These delightful blooms are produced in summer and will last for four to five weeks. Note the contrast of the unadorned sepals with the frilled petals and flared lip.

FLOWER SIZE: 4 INCHES (10CM) ACROSS
PLANT HEIGHT: 14 INCHES (35CM)
POT SIZE: 6 INCHES (15CM)

PAPHIOPEDILUM MAUDIAE

This delightful hybrid exhibits the
clear, clean lines that have made it
a classic among the green-flowered
slipper orchids. Raised in Britain
in 1900 from two green varieties
of species (*P. callosum* and
P. lawrenceanum) from Thailand and
Borneo, the result has stood the test
of time and is as popular today as
ever. The blooms will last for two
months and generally appear during
the fall and early winter. The plant
has attractive mottled green foliage,
with rounded-oval leaves. At one
time, along with many other similar
varieties, it was grown extensively
for the cut-flower trade but now
it has become more popular as
a houseplant. Grow in a shady
room, out of any direct sun
and in intermediate temperatures.

FLOWER SIZE: 4 INCHES (10CM) ACROSS
FLOWER SPIKE: 1 FOOT (30CM)
PLANT SPREAD: 10 INCHES (25CM)
POT SIZE: 4 INCHES (10CM)

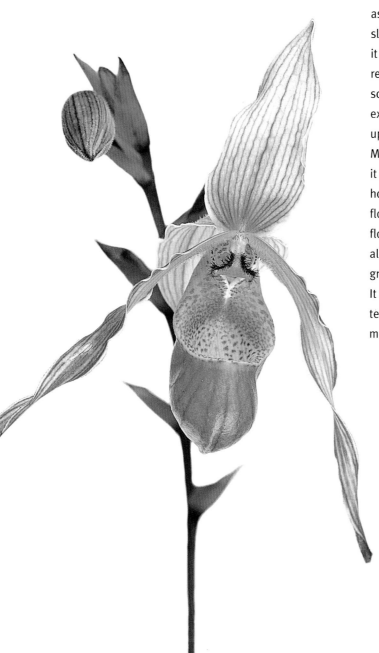

PHRAGMIPEDIUM PATTI MACHALE

This slipper orchid is a 1950's
American hybrid. It is also known
as the mandarin orchid, for its long,
slanting petals. A handsome flower,
it has received much attention and
renewed interest recently. While
some phragmipediums can become
extremely tall, with flower spikes
up to 40 inches (1m) long, *P.* Patti
MacHale is more compact, making
it easy to accommodate as a
houseplant. It has an extended
flowering period, producing one
flower at a time in sequence for
almost a year. The plant has tufted
growths, lacking pseudobulbs.
It will grow easily in intermediate
temperatures, and should be kept
moist all year round.

FLOWER SIZE: 4 INCHES (10CM) LONG
FLOWER SPIKE: 1¹⁄₂–2 FEET (45–60CM)
PLANT HEIGHT: 9 INCHES (23CM)
POT SIZE: 4–6 INCHES (10–15CM)

PAPHIOPEDILUM SPICERIANUM

Today this Himalayan species is rare, both in the wild and in cultivation, and is found only in specialist collections, but there are a multitude of hybrids available from it. Since its introduction in 1878, when it was named in honor of the grower Herbert Spicer of Surrey, England, it has been used extensively for breeding. The species has oblong green leaves and produces flower spikes with a single green-copper bloom that will last for up to three months during the fall and winter. The dorsal petal is hooded, which in the wild prevents water from entering the pouch. Water droplets look attractive, as in the photograph on the left, but they can cause damp spots or even bud drop, therefore when misting, be careful to spray only the leaves. This orchid requires cool conditions—a cool windowsill will do—and water all year round. It can be grown on to produce a large specimen with multiple flowers.

FLOWER SIZE: 3 INCHES (8CM) ACROSS
FLOWER SPIKE: 7 INCHES (18CM)
PLANT SPREAD: 10 INCHES (25CM)
POT SIZE: 6 INCHES (15CM)

PAPHIOPEDILUM LEEANUM

This plant is an orchid classic—
a very old primary hybrid raised
in Britain in 1884, when the first
hybrids were appearing among the
orchids. From the start, these
handsome slipper orchids were in the
forefront of this new hybridizing and
were among the most popular with
the (mostly gentlemen) growers of
that time. The parents of this
lovely hybrid are *P. insigne* and
P. spicerianum, two of the most
popular orchids of their time, and
even today they are both
considered to be collectables.
Once extremely plentiful, they are
now rare in collections, as is the
hybrid from them. This plant
exhibits all the grace and classic
lines of the species. It should be
grown in cool, shady conditions
and blooms in winter. The single
blooms will last for eight weeks
or more.

FLOWER SIZE: 3 INCHES (8CM) ACROSS
FLOWER SPIKE: 9 INCHES (23CM)
PLANT HEIGHT: 6 INCHES (15CM)
POT SIZE: 5 INCHES (12CM)

Paphiopedilum hirsutissimum

An old favorite, this orchid was first imported from its native India in 1857. Since that time it has remained very popular for its ease of growing and free-flowering habit. The blooms, which last for eight weeks over the winter, are large and attractively colored. The broad, pink-tipped petals are held horizontally to the small, heavily peppered dorsal petal and pouch. The stem of this species is hairy, which gives rise to the name *hirsutissimum*. The plant thrives in cool conditions, and will grow to a good size over a number of years.

Flower size: 5 inches (12cm) across
Flower spike: 9 inches (23cm)
Plant height: 6 inches (15cm)
Pot size: 5 inches (12cm)

MAXILLARIA PRAESTANS

These little winged flowers resemble a flight of strange beetles, their bodies formed by the almost black lip. They are produced singly in summer from around the base of the pseudobulbs, and on a large plant there can be a dozen or more lasting three weeks. The petals are held close to the column (see page 7), while the lateral sepals sweep down and away to give the unusual appearance of flying. This species, discovered in 1840, is found in several countries of South America, where it grows on trees as an epiphyte. The plants produce one, narrowly oval leaf from each pseudobulb, which is just taller than the flowers. The blooms are slightly fragrant at midday.

FLOWER SIZE: 2¹/₂ INCHES (6CM) ACROSS
FLOWER SPIKE: 6 INCHES (15CM)
PLANT HEIGHT: 1 FOOT (30CM)
POT SIZE: 5 INCHES (12CM)

PAPHIOPEDILUM KING ARTHUR 'BURGOYNE'

An ideal slipper orchid for the windowsill, with attractive, lightly mottled foliage that is spotted purple at the base, this is one of the oldest red hybrids, raised in Britain in 1915 and still going strong today. The flowers are glossy red and will last for a good six weeks or more in perfect condition. The single-flowered spikes appear from the center of the latest mature growth during late summer, and at some stage will require the support of a thin cane to keep them upright. The plant, which does not produce pseudobulbs, is a robust grower and will divide easily every three to four years, unless a large specimen is preferred. Keep shaded in a cool to intermediate temperatures.

FLOWER SIZE: 5 INCHES (12CM) ACROSS
FLOWER SPIKE: 9 INCHES (23CM)
PLANT SPREAD: 10 INCHES (25CM)
POT SIZE: 5 INCHES (12CM)

PAPHIOPEDILUM DELOPHYLLUM

Two distinct species, *P. delenatii* from Vietnam and *P. glaucophyllum* from Malaysia, are combined in this old primary hybrid, which was first raised in Britain in 1940. The plant is a robust grower that does best in intermediate temperatures with no direct sun. The blooms—which appear in succession on the spike, greatly extending the flowering season—are produced mainly in the winter, when individually they will last for six weeks. The plant produces attractive slightly mottled green foliage and can be divided when large enough. Always keep it in as small a pot as possible: in common with all paphiopedilums, these orchids make scanty root systems, and if overpotted there is a risk of overwatering.

FLOWER SIZE: 4 INCHES (10CM) ACROSS
FLOWER SPIKE: 1 FOOT (30CM)
PLANT HEIGHT: 4 INCHES (10CM)
POT SIZE: 3 INCHES (8CM)

CALANTHE PRINSESSE ALEXANDRA

This new hybrid, raised in Denmark and registered in 1997, is the result of crossing the species *C. rosea* with a modern hybrid, *C.* Grouville. The flower exhibits many of the characteristics of the species, with its light pink, soft-textured blooms on a long, arching flower spike. The flowers last for many weeks over the winter period, with the spike extending to provide a succession of blooms. The plant needs to be grown in warm conditions during the summer to accommodate its fast-growing habit. The silver-gray pseudobulbs do not live as long as in other orchids, and will have shriveled and died after two years, leaving only the newest one to grow and perpetuate the plant. When repotting the plant in spring, divide the pseudobulbs singly and place them together in one large pot for best effect.

FLOWER SIZE: 1$^1/_2$ INCHES (4CM) ACROSS
FLOWER SPIKE: 28 INCHES (70CM)
PLANT HEIGHT: 2 FEET (60CM)
POT SIZE: 5 INCHES (12CM)

OERSTEDELLA CENTRADENIA

This delightful little species from central South America, whose genus was first described in 1852, is just one example of how some of the smallest orchids can be so appealing and worth growing alongside the larger, more flamboyant types. Plants of this stature take up little room and can be a real boon where space is limited. You could also try growing this species in a cool, disused fish tank, where you can create a humid environment by placing pebbles in the base and keeping them wet. This is a neat plant with slender, cane-like stems and narrow leaves. The flowers are borne in spring on a spike at the top of the mature cane, with up to six flowers to a spike that will last for about three weeks.

FLOWER SIZE: $^1/_2$ INCH (1CM) ACROSS
FLOWER SPIKE: 4 INCHES (10CM)
PLANT HEIGHT: 6 INCHES (15CM)
POT SIZE: $2^1/_2$ INCHES (6CM)

BARKERIA LINDLEYANA

There are many delightful
miniature orchids that will
grace any collection, taking up
very little space on a windowsill.
This species from Guatemala,
discovered in 1842, is one of them.
In its native habitat it can be found
growing on trees or rocks, where
it will develop into quite a large
plant. In cultivation, however,
it remains compact, producing
its small stem-like growths and
up to six delightful deep cerise,
yellow-centered flowers on a
slender flower spike above the
foliage. Provide shade and
moisture to encourage the
production of thick aerial roots
in early summer. The blooms
will last for two to three weeks
in the fall.

FLOWER SIZE: 1^{1}/$_{2}$ INCHES (4CM) ACROSS
FLOWER SPIKE: 6 INCHES (15CM)
PLANT HEIGHT: 5 INCHES (12CM)
POT SIZE: 4 INCHES (10CM)

Epidendrum radicans 'Yellow'

Originally from tropical America, this widespread species was collected by the famous explorer Baron von Humboldt in 1815. It grows in the ground or on rocks, and in cultivation can be used as a bedding plant. Grown this way in the tropics, it can assume very large proportions and become extremely tall. Its flower spikes carry numerous blooms in succession over a period of many months. The plant has a reed-type habit, flowering from the mature canes at any time. Its popularity has soared in recent years with the introduction of "compact" varieties, which bloom on shorter canes but will eventually grow much taller. The shape of the flowers gives rise to its common name of crucifix orchid.

Flower size: 1 inch (2.5cm) across
Flower spike: 1–1¹/₂ feet (30–45cm)
Plant height: 40 inches (1m) eventually
Pot size: 6 inches (15cm)

EPIDENDRUM RADICANS
VAR. ALBA

This is the naturally albino form of the species, which in the type has red flowers. This variety is one of a number of color forms of this variable species. It is most often sold under the above name, although botanically it is described as *E. ibaguense*. The plant carries twenty to twenty-five white flowers on each dense head held at the end of a spike well above the foliage. The foliage is somewhat shorter and less prolific than in the type. Like *E. radicans* 'Yellow,' it can be grown as a bedding plant. Alternatively, it can be planted in a hanging basket where, in time, the new canes will assume a pendent habit and form a most graceful specimen, with numerous aerial roots extending from the plant to over 40 inches (1m) long. A succession of blooms means that this orchid will be in flower for several months.

FLOWER SIZE: 1 INCH (2.5CM) ACROSS
FLOWER SPIKE: 1 FOOT (30CM)
PLANT HEIGHT: 40 INCHES (1M)
POT SIZE: 6 INCHES (15CM)

DENDROCHILUM MAGNUM

This autumn-flowering, cool-growing species needs water all year and is one of a number from Malaya and the Philippine Islands. Those with white flowers are known as the silver chain orchids; this species with light yellow flowers is called a golden chain orchid. The flowers are carried on a long, slender, drooping flower spike that arises from the base of the new growth and blooms for around three weeks in the early fall. Up to eighty flowers are closely packed in two rows along the spike; in some species the inflorescence is twisted through its length. The flowers are strongly fragrant, and a large plant can produce numerous spikes. The pseudobulbs are small, supporting a single leaf. All the species are extremely popular and worth collecting. The genus was first described in 1825.

FLOWER SIZE: $^1/_2$ INCH (1CM) ACROSS
FLOWER SPIKE: $2^1/_2$ FEET (75CM)
PLANT HEIGHT: 1 FOOT (30CM)
POT SIZE: 6 INCHES (15CM)

BRASSADA ORANGE DELIGHT

This superb hybrid was raised in California in 1989. It brings together the qualities of *Ada* and *Brassia*, two related genera that were first used to produce the bigeneric genus *Brassada* in 1970. The coloring of this unique clone comes from *A. aurantiaca*, an orange-flowered species from South America, while its narrow, pointed sepals and petals are a contribution from the brassias—the spider orchids famed for their incredibly long sepals and petals. The plant is similar to an *Odontoglossum*, but has more elongated, neat pseudobulbs. The breeding behind this hybrid allows it to be grown in cool conditions, although in warmer climates it will tolerate higher temperatures. It also likes to be kept moist and shaded. The plant is summer flowering, and the blooms, up to six or eight on a spike, will last four to five weeks.

FLOWER SIZE: $3^1/_2$ INCHES (9CM) LONG
FLOWER SPIKE: 16 INCHES (40CM)
PLANT HEIGHT: 1 FOOT (30CM)
POT SIZE: 4 INCHES (10CM)

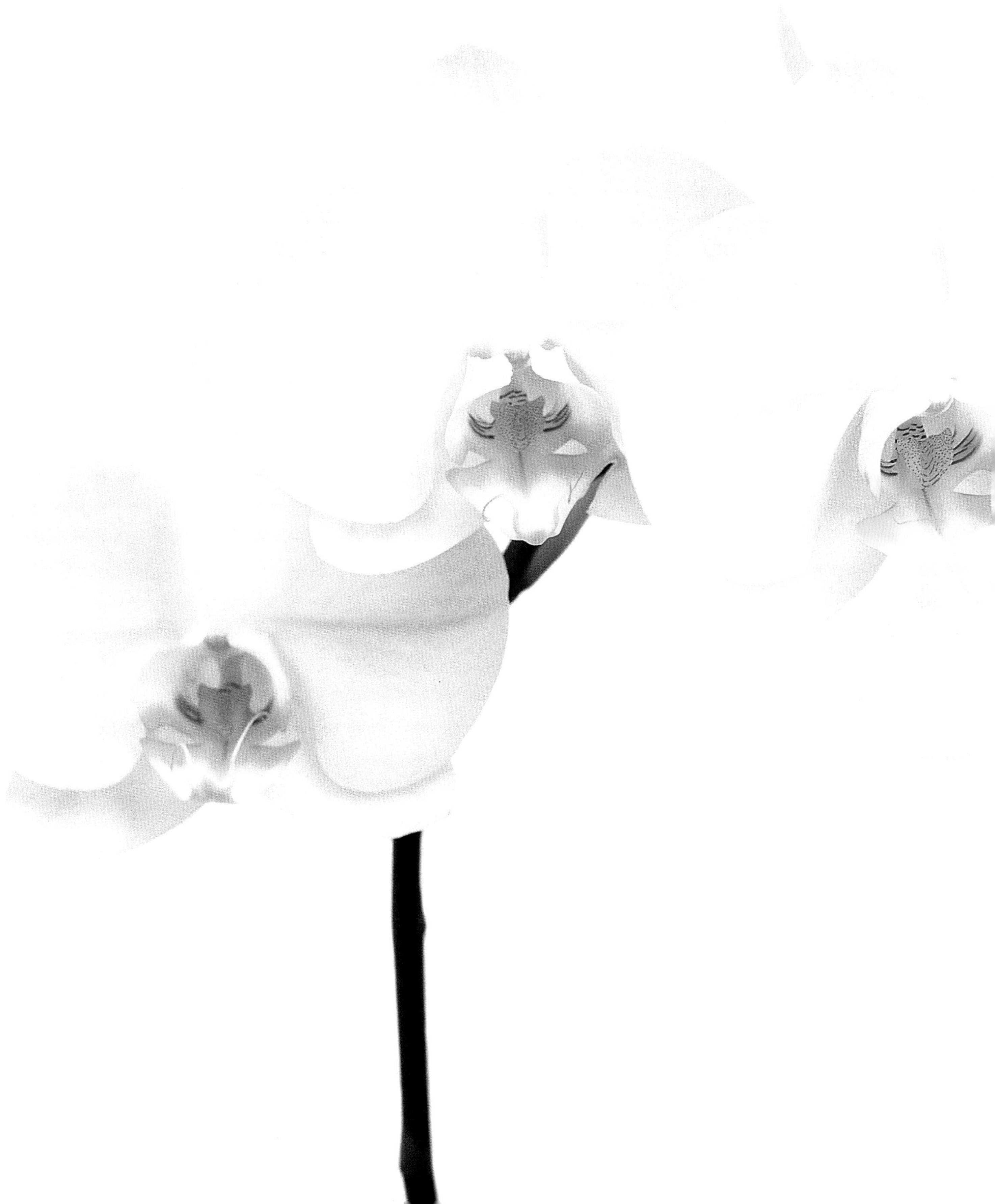

PHALAENOPSIS AMABILIS

This is one of the species that has been used to create so many of the modern hybrids. Originating from the Philippine Islands where it was discovered in 1750, it has been a favorite for well over a century. Today's plants are the result of cross-breeding different clones over many years to improve the strain. Their size and shape have become more rounded than in the original importations. The leaves of this species are light green, but otherwise indistinguishable from those of the hybrids. The flower has a simple purity that ensures it will always have a place in collections. In the wild, the plants grow upon trees, with their leaves and flower spikes—bearing six to eighteen flowers per spike in summer—drooping downward and with the flowers held clear of the branches.

FLOWER SIZE: 3½ INCHES (9CM) ACROSS
FLOWER SPIKE: 15 INCHES (38CM)
PLANT SPREAD: 1 FOOT (30CM)
POT SIZE: 5 INCHES (12CM)

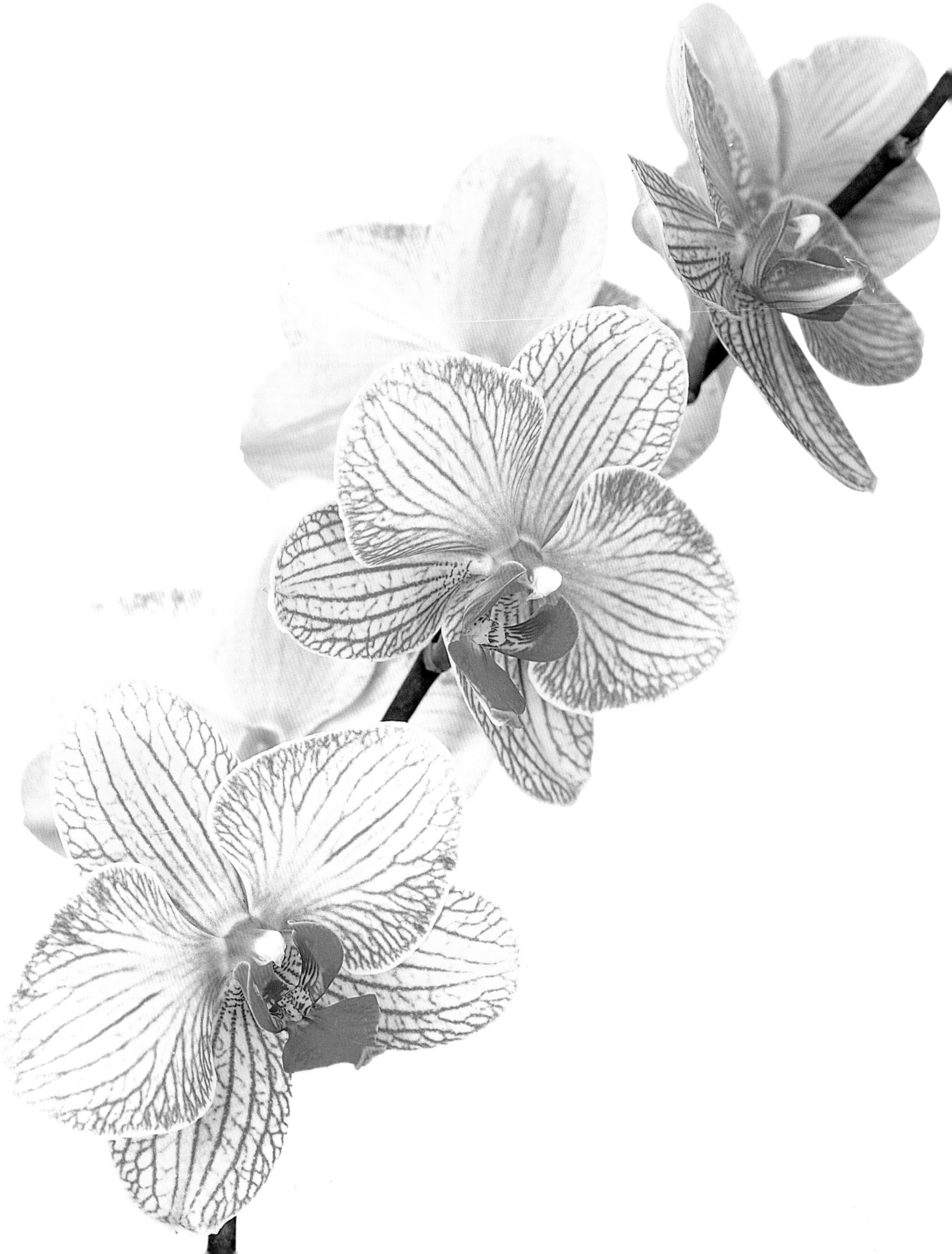

PHALAENOPSIS MIVA GOLDEN 'MAJESTIC'

This new, French-bred hybrid raised in 1991 derives its name from its parents—P. Golden Horizon, the yellow parent and P. Miva Smartissimo, the pink parent. It is a delightful flower, showing the rich color and overall veining and spotting that is characteristic of this type. 'Majestic' is a robust plant, without pseudobulbs, which will bloom two to three times a year in any season. Six to seven flowers lasting six to eight weeks are carried on an arching spike well above the foliage. Cut down the flower spike to a lower node after flowering and a second spike will then grow to give more flowers.

FLOWER SIZE: 3$^{1}/_{2}$ INCHES (9CM) ACROSS
FLOWER SPIKE: 2 FEET (60CM)
PLANT SPREAD: 1 FOOT (30CM)
POT SIZE: 5 INCHES (12CM)

PHALAENOPSIS BROTHER LANCER

Taiwan has become the home of a large number of very fine *Phalaenopsis* hybrids produced to a high standard for the pot-plant trade. In addition to the more usual pink and white varieties, there are some extremely attractive patterned clones, such as P. Brother Lancer which was introduced in 1995. Here, selected breeding lines have produced a beautifully veined and striped flower, rich red on a pale background, and with a cherry-red lip. Up to eight blooms to a spike can be expected, held well above the foliage at almost any time of the year and lasting for seven to eight weeks. Grow on a warm, shady windowsill or similar position, and keep watered throughout the year.

FLOWER SIZE: 3$^{1}/_{2}$ INCHES (9CM) ACROSS
FLOWER SPIKE: 10 INCHES (25CM)
PLANT SPREAD: 9 INCHES (23CM)
POT SIZE: 5 INCHES (12CM)

DORITIS PULCHERRIMA 'ROSEA'

A miniature species discovered in Malaya in 1833, this plant resembles *Phalaenopsis* in growth and will interbreed with this genus to produce the very colorful *Doritaenopsis*. The vivid coloring of the small flowers, which are carried up to a dozen at a time on an upright flower spike, can be seen very clearly in this variety. The species is extremely variable, with white and pink forms also known. It also has a tendency to repeat the lip patterning on the lateral petals, a form known as peloric, as seen here. This attractive, compact plant must be grown in warm conditions and kept moist all year round.

FLOWER SIZE: 1½ INCHES (4CM) ACROSS
FLOWER SPIKE: 6 INCHES (15CM)
PLANT SPREAD: 3–4 INCHES (8–10CM)
POT SIZE: 4 INCHES (10CM)

DORITAENOPSIS CORAL HARBOR

This is a bigeneric hybrid, the result of crossing *Phalaenopsis* with *Doritis*. Here the *Phalaenopsis* side is dominant, the small percentage of *Doritis* genes showing in the vigor of the plant and the richness of the deeply colored lip. This hybrid was raised in California in 1991 and is one of many successful similar clones. Note that the flower spike, bearing up to a dozen blooms, arches over and will need to be tied to a supporting cane just below the first flowers. The blooms can appear at any time of year and will last for seven to eight weeks. Lacking pseudobulbs, this plant must be watered throughout the year and should be grown in a warm room well out of direct sun. It could also be grown in a shaded greenhouse.

FLOWER SIZE: 3$\frac{1}{2}$ INCHES (9CM) ACROSS
FLOWER SPIKE: 1$\frac{1}{2}$–2 FEET (45–60CM)
PLANT SPREAD: 1 FOOT (30CM)
POT SIZE: 5 INCHES (12CM)

PHALAENOPSIS HAPPY GIRL

This is the classic hybrid, bred in 1994 in Taiwan. It has neatly arching flower spikes and up to a dozen blooms with overlapping petals. These tall spikes will need extra support to prevent them from kinking under their own weight. The plant is robust, with the broad, thick leaves that are typical of the genus and with aerial roots that prefer to remain outside the pot. When the plant is large enough it will seldom be out of flower. You can extend the flowering by cutting back the stem to a lower node immediately after the first flush. This will encourage more branching. This variety is also very popular for floral displays.

FLOWER SIZE: 4 INCHES (10CM) ACROSS
FLOWER SPIKE: 20 INCHES (50CM)
PLANT SPREAD: 14 INCHES (35CM)
POT SIZE: 5 INCHES (12CM)

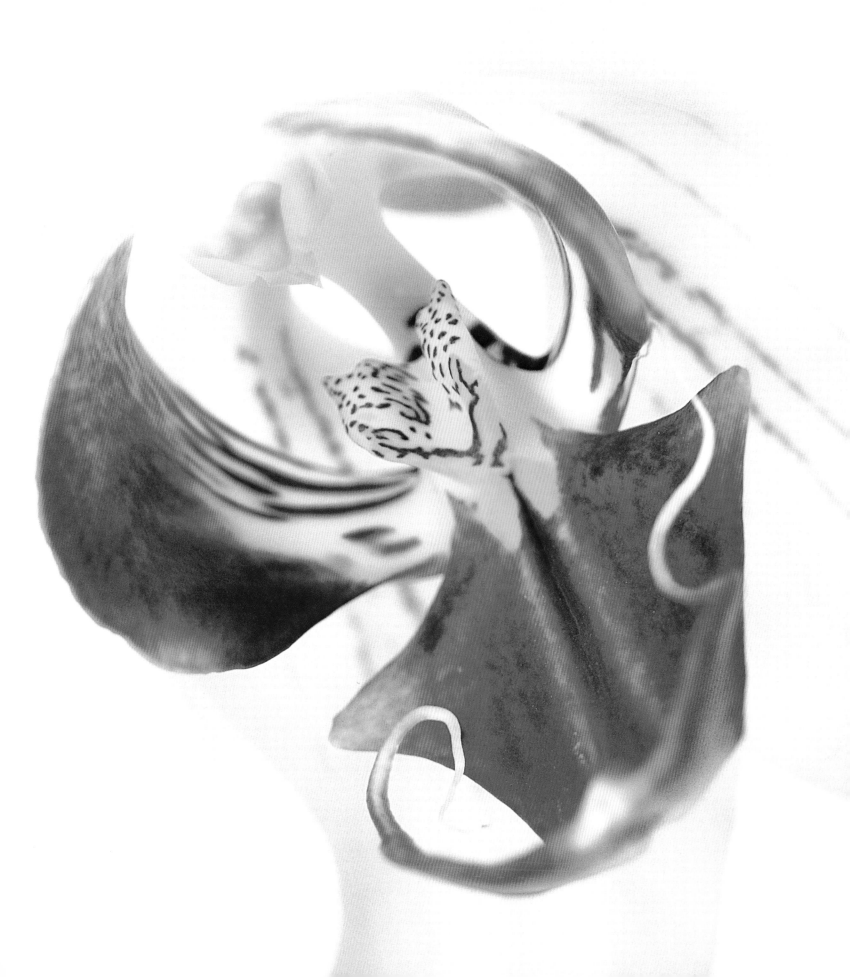

Phalaenopsis Brother Golden Potential

This fabulous moth orchid was produced in Taiwan in 1998, the result of a long line of specialist breeding that brought out the sought-after qualities of rich, sunshine-yellow coloring combined with a well-rounded shape. Since it first appeared, this outstanding hybrid has been mass-produced and is now grown worldwide. The exciting blooms—six to eight borne on branching spikes two or three times a year—are slightly smaller than in many of the white- and pink-flowered varieties. The plant is also compact, consisting of only three or four leaves at any one time. Ideal as houseplants, these orchids require warm conditions and shade. Keep them watered throughout the year.

Flower size: 3 inches (8cm) across
Flower spike: 1½–2 feet (45–60cm)
Plant spread: 7 inches (18cm)
Pot size: 5 inches (12cm)

PHALAENOPSIS VANILLY

Although this flower, raised in 1999, is not as large as in some of the truly huge white varieties, its blooms are produced on a semi-upright flower spike. The ivory-white blooms, their lower petals lightly spotted at the base, owe much to the species *P. stuartiana*, which comes from the Philippine Islands and passes on the tell-tale spotting. Other varieties have gone into this hybrid to create a lovely combination with a colorful red lip. The spike usually bears up to five flowers, which will last for six weeks and can be produced at any time of the year.

FLOWER SIZE: 4 INCHES (10CM) ACROSS
FLOWER SPIKE: 20 INCHES (50CM)
PLANT SPREAD: 14 INCHES (35CM)
POT SIZE: 5 INCHES (12CM)

Coelogyne cristata

This is one of the most favored orchid species of all time. Plants in cultivation today can often be traced to importations from India dating back to 1822. A strong, robust grower, within a few years it can assume gigantic proportions. However, continual division of the plant will maintain it at a manageable level. A large plant positively froths with big, crisp white blooms, which are produced freely in early spring and last three to four weeks. On a sizeable plant, a slight fragrance can be detected. Grow it in cool conditions, in good light all winter. In early spring the flower spikes, with up to six blooms to a spike, will show from the base of the mature pseudobulbs. The developing buds start off looking brownish. Just when you think they are dying off, they change to glistening white, prior to opening in all their glory.

Flower size: 3 inches (8cm) across
Flower spike: 6 inches (15cm)
Plant height: 10 inches (25cm) plus
Pot size: 4 inches (10cm)

ONCIDIUM TWINKLE

This delightful primary hybrid was
raised in Britain in 1958 as a result
of crossing two epiphytic species—
O. ornithorhynchum and
O. cheirophorum. The former is
pink flowered and the latter yellow;
both are delightfully aromatic. The
hybrid has inherited the fragrance,
and its coloring is between that
of the two parents. The plant,
while vigorous and extremely
free flowering, is compact with
small pseudobulbs and short foliage.
It regularly produces two or three
flower spikes from one pseudobulb
during the fall. These are packed
with dozens of delicate flowers, and
on a large plant they can be counted
in the hundreds. Because the blooms
do not open all at the same time,
the flowering season is extended
over several weeks. Position
on a cool, shady windowsill for
optimum growth.

FLOWER SIZE: 1/2 INCH (1CM) ACROSS
FLOWER SPIKE: 1 FOOT (30CM)
PLANT HEIGHT: 6 INCHES (15CM)
POT SIZE: 4 INCHES (10CM)

ONCIDIUM ALOHA IWANAGA 'HAWAIIAN GEM'

Three golden yellow species—
O. flexuosum, O. sphacelatum, and
O. varicosum—combine their best
qualities to produce this excellent,
brilliantly colored Hawaiian hybrid,
bred in 1990. The delightful flowers,
commonly called dancing ladies, are
carried on side branches to the main
stem, each bearing fifty to eighty
blooms that last for three to four weeks
in summer. This orchid, which produces
pseudobulbs, is very easy to grow in
most climates and is a popular
houseplant. It is also grown extensively
for cut flowers. Its long, attractive
sprays look stunning in flower
arrangements.

FLOWER SIZE: 1 INCH (2.5CM) ACROSS
FLOWER SPIKE: 25 INCHES (63CM)
PLANT HEIGHT: 1 FOOT (30CM)
POT SIZE: 6 INCHES (15CM)

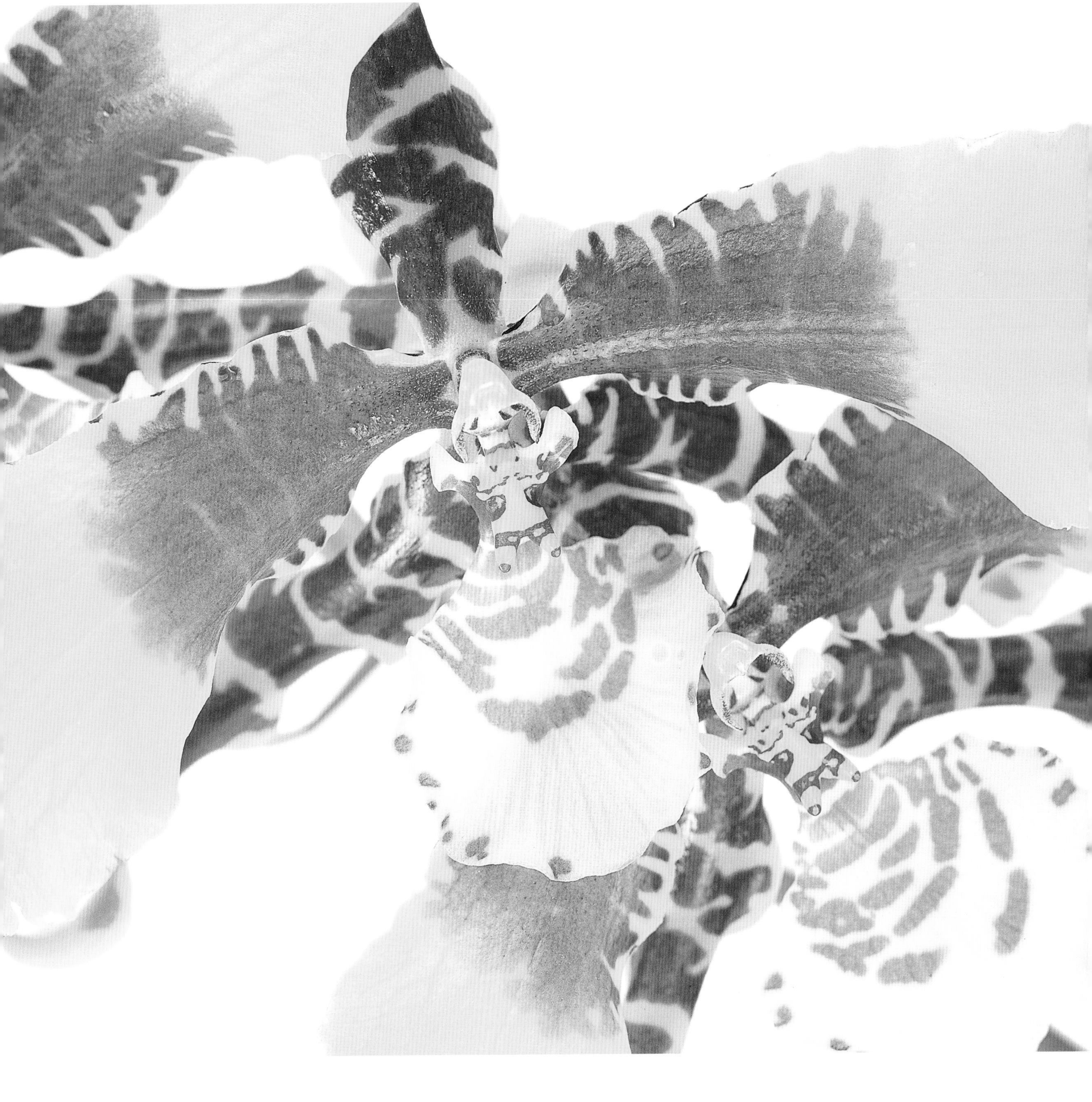

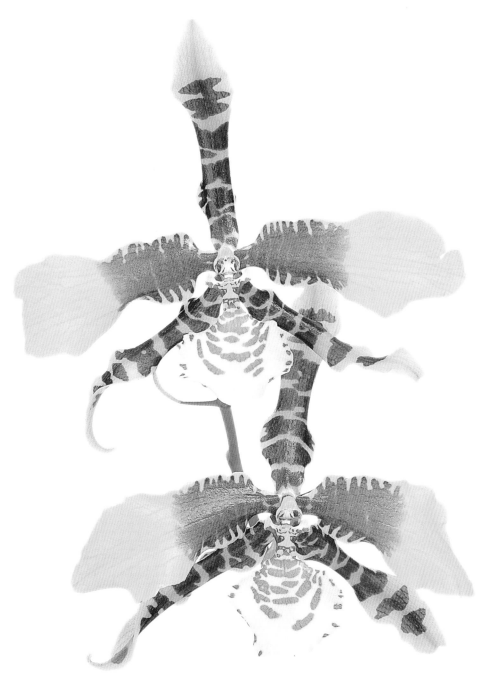

ROSSIOGLOSSUM RAWDON JESTER

This amazing hybrid produces large, glossy, eye-catching flowers during the summer months. It is a primary hybrid raised in Britain in 1983 from two similar species, *R. grande* and *R. williamsianum*, both originating from Guatemala. These were originally classified under *Odontoglossum* and are now rare in cultivation, which makes this hybrid even more desirable. The upright flower spikes carry four to six blooms that will last three to four weeks. The plant is strong and robust, and is an easy orchid to grow indoors. It has attractive, dark green foliage with large pseudobulbs.

FLOWER SIZE: 6 INCHES (15CM) ACROSS
FLOWER SPIKE: 20 INCHES (50CM)
PLANT HEIGHT: 6 INCHES (15CM)
POT SIZE: 8 INCHES (20CM)

ODONTIODA QUEDLINBURG

An exquisitely patterned hybrid raised in Germany in 1997, this orchid is favored for its primrose-yellow flowers overlaid with colorful red markings as if from an artist's brush. Although this is an *Odontioda* hybrid, which contains genes from *Cochlioda* that usually impart a rich red coloring, in this instance more influence has been exerted by the *Odontoglossum* side, which the flowers resemble more closely. The plant is typical of the latter, with neat pseudobulbs and two long, narrow leaves. The spikes are taller than the foliage and can each carry up to eight good-size flowers. These will bloom at various times of year, but mainly during the summer months when they will last for around six weeks.

FLOWER SIZE: 3¹/₂ INCHES (9CM) ACROSS
FLOWER SPIKE: 27 INCHES (68CM)
PLANT HEIGHT: 14 INCHES (35CM)
POT SIZE: 5 INCHES (12CM)

DENDROBIUM STARDUST 'CHYOMI'

This gorgeous hybrid is a soft-caned *Dendrobium*, originally bred from the species *D. nobile* which originates from India and Nepal. *D.* Stardust was raised in 1986 by a Japanese nursery in Hawaii; the hybrids come in a wide range of flamboyant colors and produce their flowers on short stems along the length of the elongated pseudobulbs, otherwise known as canes. The blooms last roughly four weeks and appear in early spring following the plant's winter rest. During this rest, the plant should be kept dry until the buds are seen. Keep these orchids cool and in full light during the rest period, but provide warmer conditions by moving them to a shadier aspect after flowering when their long canes immediately start to grow.

FLOWER SIZE: 2¹/₂ INCHES (6CM) ACROSS
PLANT HEIGHT: 1 FOOT (30CM)
POT SIZE: 4¹/₂ INCHES (11CM)

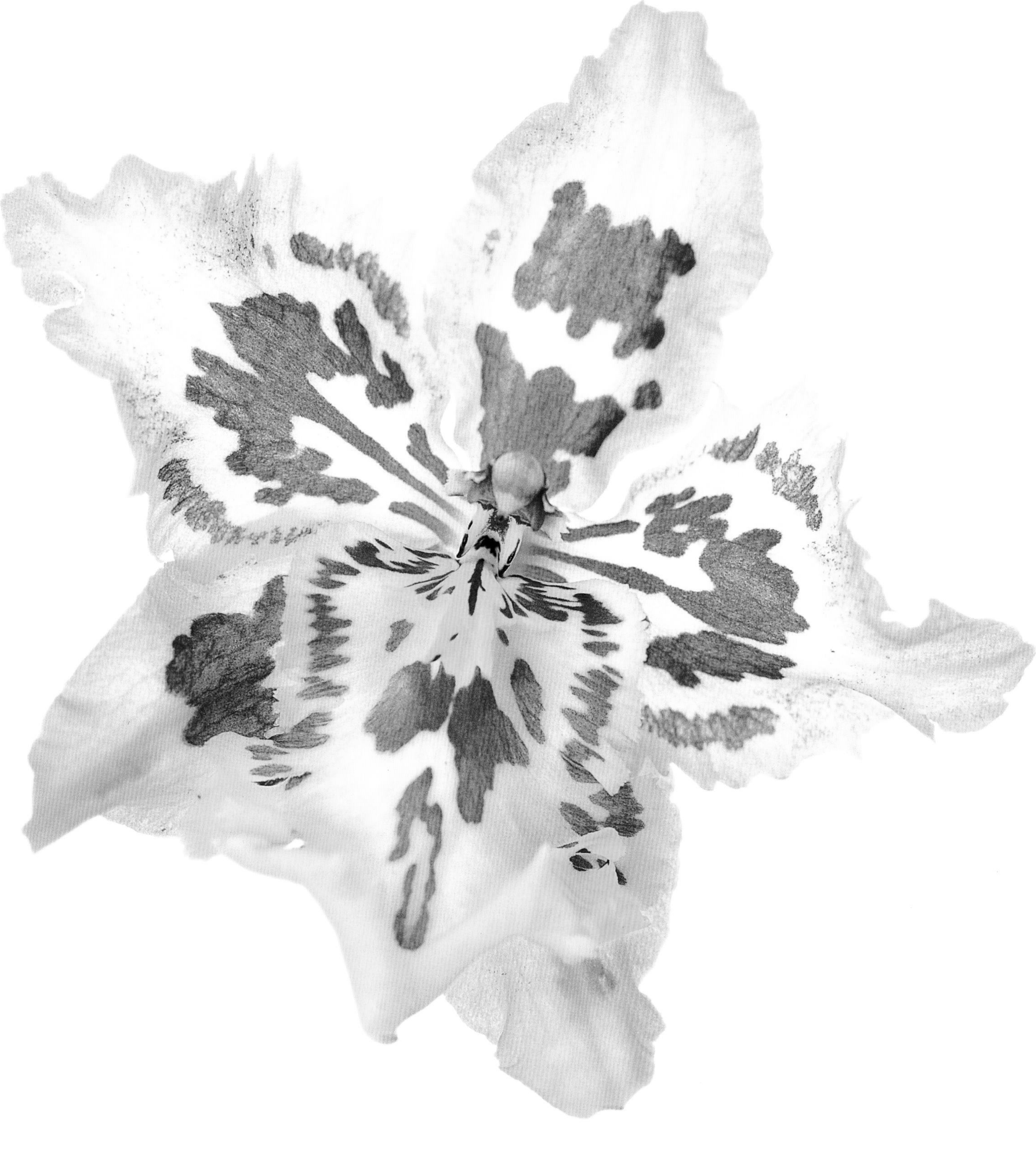

LEMBOGLOSSUM BICTONIENSE

Once included in the genus *Odontoglossum*, this handsome species from Guatemala was introduced into cultivation in 1835 and first flowered at Bicton in Devon, England. It produces green pseudobulbs and makes an attractive, easily grown plant that blooms freely during the summer.

As it matures, two flower spikes, each bearing twelve to fifteen flowers, are often carried by one pseudobulb. The flowers have narrow green sepals and petals barred with brown, and a white to pink heart-shaped lip. They will last for four to five weeks. The best clones have produced some very desirable hybrids.

FLOWER SIZE: 1¹/₂ INCHES (4CM) ACROSS
FLOWER SPIKE: 2¹/₂ FEET (75CM)
PLANT HEIGHT: 10 INCHES (25CM)
POT SIZE: 5 INCHES (12CM)

LEMBOGLOSSUM VIOLETTA VON HOLM 'WILMA'

This hybrid, formerly classified under *Odontoglossum*, was bred in Germany in 1994 from the species *L. bictoniense* and *L. rossii*, which gives *L.* Bic-Ross, and crossed back onto *L. bictoniense*. There are numerous clones available, the best of which is 'Wilma,' a charming, compact, free-flowering plant that is easy to grow. It requires cool, airy conditions—a cool windowsill is perfect. If it is too warm it will only survive for a short time. The plant produces small pseudobulbs and blooms mostly in the spring, when the flowers—as many as twelve to eighteen to a spike—will last for up to six weeks.

FLOWER SIZE: 2 INCHES (5CM) ACROSS
FLOWER SPIKE: 1¹/₂–2 FEET (45–60CM)
PLANT HEIGHT: 6 INCHES (15CM)
POT SIZE: 4¹/₂–5 INCHES (11–12CM)

VUYLSTEKEARA CAMBRIA 'LENSING'S FAVORIT'

An embellished variation raised in Britain in 1931 on the more usual *V.* Cambria clone, this delicately patterned form has much to commend it. It comes from one of the most popular hybrids of all time and is renowned for its ease of culture and ability to grow and flower under a range of conditions, although it does best on a cool windowsill out of direct sun.
This is a complex hybrid with *Odontoglossum*, *Cochlioda*, and *Miltonia* all involved. It is a strong grower with a neat habit, similar to an *Odontoglossum*. It will bloom freely at almost any time of the year with six to twelve flowers per spike lasting five or six weeks. This is one orchid with which you cannot go far wrong.

FLOWER SIZE: 3 INCHES (8CM) ACROSS
FLOWER SPIKE: 2 FEET (60CM)
PLANT HEIGHT: 16 INCHES (40CM)
POT SIZE: 5 INCHES (12CM)

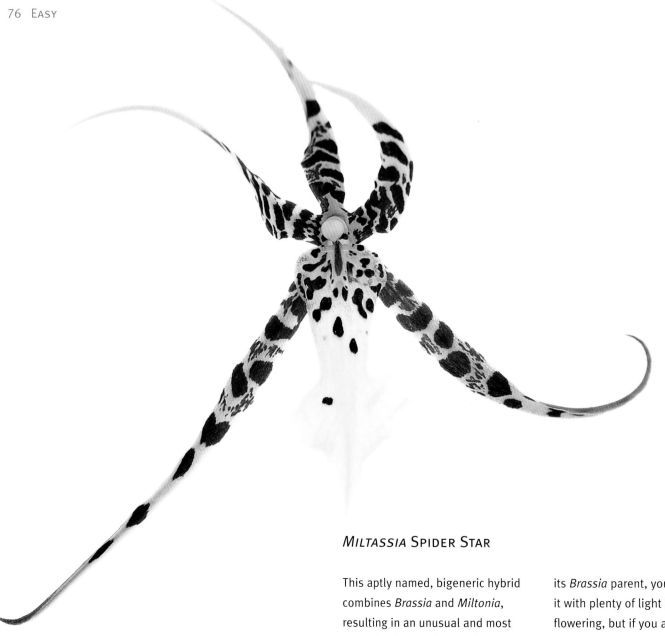

MILTASSIA SPIDER STAR

This aptly named, bigeneric hybrid combines *Brassia* and *Miltonia*, resulting in an unusual and most attractive flower sharing the shape of the former (commonly called spider orchids) and the leopard patterning of the latter. This vigorous hybrid is tolerant of a wide range of temperatures and can be acclimatized to grow in both cool and warm conditions. Because of its *Brassia* parent, you must provide it with plenty of light to encourage flowering, but if you are growing it in a greenhouse, be careful not to allow full sun to scorch the leaves. The plant produces pseudobulbs and flowers during spring and summer, and the flower spikes consist of six to eight blooms that will last for four to five weeks.

FLOWER SIZE: 4½ INCHES (11CM) ACROSS
FLOWER SPIKE: 15–20 INCHES (38–50CM)
PLANT HEIGHT: 9 INCHES (23CM)
POT SIZE: 5 INCHES (12CM)

MILTASSIA CAIRNS

Raised in 1991, this fabulous new variety has large, dominant flowers brightly patterned in contrasting rich red and mauve. It is a bigeneric hybrid combining *Miltonia* and *Brassia*. The former has contributed to the outstanding coloring, while the latter has narrowed and lengthened the petals and sepals, to give a starry shape. This winning combination is displayed in two to three flowers per spike, which stands well clear of the foliage. The blooms are produced in summer, when they will last for five weeks. The plant resembles an *Odontoglossum* but is larger and more robust, and two flower spikes per pseudobulb is usual. Grow *M.* Cairns in intermediate orchid conditions (see page 120), where it will thrive in a shady position, but take care not to provide too much light as this will spoil the foliage.

FLOWER SIZE: 3 INCHES (8CM) ACROSS
FLOWER SPIKE: 14 INCHES (35CM)
PLANT HEIGHT: 1 FOOT (30CM)
POT SIZE: 8 INCHES (20CM)

BRASSIA ARANIA VERDE

The brassias are the well-known
spider orchids, so called for their
extraordinarily long, thin petals and
sepals, which are held out stiffly. The lip
is large by comparison, but also narrow
and pointed. The flowers are extremely
fragrant and are produced in long
sprays of up to ten blooms. They are
largely green, as seen here, with rich
chocolate-brown barring along the
petals and sepals. The plant resembles
an *Odontoglossum*, with which genus
it will interbreed, and has robust
pseudobulbs and two broadly oval
leaves. The flower spikes appear in late
spring as the pseudobulbs mature, and
the blooms will last for five to six weeks
in intermediate temperatures. This
hybrid was bred in 1990.

FLOWER SIZE: 10 INCHES (25CM) LONG
FLOWER SPIKE: 2 FEET (60CM)
PLANT HEIGHT: 20 INCHES (50CM)
POT SIZE: 7 INCHES (18CM)

PHOLIDOTA RUBRA

This intriguing miniature species
discovered in India in 1836 is known
as the rattlesnake orchid for the
shape of its pendent inflorescence
that gives the impression of a
rattlesnake's tail. The individual
cupped and rounded flowers appear
in the fall and are densely packed
along the drooping spike. They are
extremely small and do not open
fully. This is one of very many
miniature orchids which find favor
with lovers of small, unusual plants.
The plant itself is neat, with rounded
pseudobulbs and a single leaf on
each. From the base of this, the
flower spike extends from an
extremely thin and wiry stem.
The plant does well with very little
attention on a windowsill or in a
cool greenhouse.

FLOWER SIZE: ¹/₄ INCH (5MM) ACROSS
FLOWER SPIKE: 7 INCHES (18CM)
PLANT HEIGHT: 9 INCHES (23CM)
POT SIZE: 3 INCHES (8CM)

DEGAMORARA KATHLEEN OKA

This modern hybrid, raised in Hawaii
in 1980, makes a large, robust plant
with very large pseudobulbs and tall
foliage. The flower spikes are also
quite long, bearing numerous
eye-catching blooms in a range of
stunning colors. They appear from
the mature pseudobulb at any time
of the year and the blooms will last
around four weeks. The plant is
a cross between *Brassia*, creating
the narrow petals and sepals, and
Odontonia, itself a cross between
Odontoglossum and *Miltonia*.
D. Kathleen Oka is therefore a
trigeneric cross, the result of the
hybridizers' skill in producing an
entirely new and unnatural hybrid.
Its vigor and tolerance enable the
plant to be grown in all climates,
from temperate to tropical.

FLOWER SIZE: 3 INCHES (8CM) ACROSS
FLOWER SPIKE: 28 INCHES (70CM)
PLANT HEIGHT: 14 INCHES (35CM)
POT SIZE: 7 INCHES (18CM)

ENCYCLIA RADIATA

This orchid will produce several new growths in a season and can be grown on into a large specimen. But it also looks charming on a windowsill, and you can easily keep it at the desired size by dividing it every few years. It flowers profusely during the summer, bearing delightful creamy-white, highly scented blooms. The flowers open with their lip held at the top, which is different than most orchids. This species, which comes from Mexico, makes slender pseudobulbs with a pair of narrow mid-green leaves. The flowers, six or eight to a spike, will last for five to six weeks.

FLOWER SIZE: $1^{1}/_{2}$ INCHES (4CM) ACROSS
FLOWER SPIKE: 4 INCHES (10CM)
PLANT HEIGHT: 10 INCHES (25CM)
POT SIZE: 6 INCHES (15CM)

ENCYCLIA FAUSTA

Discovered in Brazil in 1827, this
is a delightful small species that
produces sprays of pretty, fragrant
white flowers with a red-lined lip.
It is one of a group of similar species,
all of which are worth collecting for
their fragrant, early summer blooms.
This one is extremely easy to grow
and will do well in either cool or
intermediate temperatures. The six
or eight blooms on each very short
spike appear from the apex of the
slender pseudobulb, and they will
last for up to six weeks. While a
young plant fits easily onto a
windowsill, within a few years it
may well have outgrown the space
available. By dividing plants every
few years you can maintain the
required size.

FLOWER SIZE: 2 INCHES (5CM) ACROSS
FLOWER SPIKE: 4 INCHES (10CM)
PLANT HEIGHT: 10 INCHES (25CM)
POT SIZE: 4 INCHES (10CM)

LYCASTE LASIOGLOSSA

This lovely, distinct species, which has been in cultivation since 1871, comes from Guatemala and has been used widely for hybridizing, contributing color to the modern hybrids. It blooms in spring, producing its sharply three-sided blooms singly on spikes held above the foliage, which is shed at about the same time as flowering commences. The outside sepals of the flowers are brown and the two lateral petals yellow, with the small central lip frilled and similarly colored. The blooms last for around five weeks. The plant enjoys cool conditions, but needs a dry winter rest following the growing season.

FLOWER SIZE: 3$\frac{1}{2}$ INCHES (9CM) ACROSS
FLOWER SPIKE: 9 INCHES (23CM)
PLANT HEIGHT: 20 INCHES (50CM)
POT SIZE: 6 INCHES (15CM)

LYCASTE SKINNERI

This species was introduced from Guatemala in 1840 by George Ure-Skinner, after whom it was named. Today, it is the national flower of that country. This is an extremely pretty and variable species that was once grown extensively in collections, and the many color forms were all collected. Today it is very rare, and it is the colorful hybrids that have been produced from it that are more often seen. The species is usually encountered under the above name, although botanically it is described as *L. virginalis*. The plant is semi-deciduous and enjoys cool conditions, with plenty of water in summer and a dry rest in winter. One flower per spike appears in spring and will last for six weeks.

FLOWER SIZE: 4 INCHES (10CM) ACROSS
FLOWER SPIKE: 8 INCHES (20CM)
PLANT HEIGHT: 1½ FEET (45CM)
POT SIZE: 4 INCHES (10CM)

Fairly easy

Our selection of orchids under the heading "fairly easy" covers those that, while suitable for a beginner, may not be quite as tolerant of less than ideal conditions as the "easy" orchids. Miltoniopsis, for example, will easily grow alongside others with similar requirements, but their paler foliage is softer and more susceptible to damage from bright sunlight. So while all orchids require some degree of shade, for miltoniopsis this is probably more important than, say, keeping to the minimum recommended temperature.

Many dendrobiums are also included in this section. They are here because they need a rest from growing during the winter months and at this time they should be kept drier. For example, if *Dendrobium nobile* is watered during early spring when its buds are developing, it may produce adventitious growths instead of flowers. However, do not despair. These can always be potted up when large enough to give you more plants!

ZYGOPETALUM LUISENDORF

Zygopetalums are becoming more and more popular as new varieties and hybrids that are easy to grow and bloom freely come onto the market. Bred from species originally imported from Brazil, the dominant colors have always been green and brown. By incorporating other species, new colors are being created to greatly extend the range and desirability. This new hybrid produces a compact plant, which blooms from the latest pseudobulb throughout the fall. The fragrant blooms, two to three at a time, are held at the end of the flower spike and will last for three to four weeks. They are light olive-brown with a large, spreading purple lip that is deeply veined and colored. Grow in cool to intermediate temperatures in a well-drained potting mix to prevent the plant from getting too wet in winter.

FLOWER SIZE: 2¹/₂ INCHES (6CM) ACROSS
FLOWER SPIKE: 1 FOOT (30CM)
PLANT HEIGHT: 10 INCHES (25CM)
POT SIZE: 5 INCHES (12CM)

ZYGOPETALUM SKIPPY KU

This is a colorful genus, gaining in popularity as modern breeding results in some new and exciting flowers. A dark-hued primary hybrid, bred in the United States in 1975, it has two distinct species for parents, *Z. graminifolium* and *Z. intermedium*, both of which come from Central America. The coloring in the hybrid displays rich indigo veining on the lip, contrasting with brown and green petals and sepals. The plants can be quite large and robust with a few, narrowly oval leaves and stout pseudobulbs. The flower spikes, with up to six blooms each, arise from the base of the new growths during the spring months and the flowers, which are fragrant, will last for three weeks. Several flower spikes can be expected from a medium-size plant. Grow in shade in intermediate temperatures.

FLOWER SIZE: 2 INCHES (5CM) ACROSS
FLOWER SPIKE: 14 INCHES (35CM)
PLANT HEIGHT: 1 FOOT (30CM)
POT SIZE: 4 INCHES (10CM)

MASDEVALLIA MAGDALENA X MARGUERITE

This exquisite hybrid shows the depth of coloring that can be achieved. It is extremely free flowering and produces its cheerful single flowers on slender spikes. While this plant can be divided regularly, it is better when left to grow into a larger specimen so that its full beauty can be realized. The cherry-red flowers will last for two to three weeks throughout summer; they display the characteristic tails on enlarged sepals which give this genus the name of kite orchids. This orchid needs the same care as *Masdevallia* Marguerite (see opposite) and *Masdevallia* Mary Staal (see page 100).

FLOWER SIZE: 1¼ INCHES (3CM) ACROSS
FLOWER SPIKE: 16 INCHES (40CM)
PLANT HEIGHT: 10 INCHES (25CM)
POT SIZE: 3–4 INCHES (8–10CM)

MASDEVALLIA MARGUERITE

This rosy-cheeked hybrid with the smiley face is one of the attractive kite orchids, so called for the long tails that adorn the sepals. It was bred in the United States in 1982. The species in this genus all come from high altitudes in the South American rain forests. Here they enjoy a climate of perpetual spring, where the day temperatures are never too high and the nights never too cold. When cultivated outside their natural habitat, species and hybrid are fairly easy to grow provided these conditions can be met. They therefore do best in a cool environment that is well shaded and humid in summer. You can ensure the humidity by growing them in a group on a humidity tray. *M.* Marguerite has short-stemmed, tufty leafed growths, and produces its flowers singly on flower spikes above the foliage throughout the summer.

FLOWER SIZE: 2^1/$_2$ INCHES (6CM) ACROSS
FLOWER SPIKE: 6 INCHES (15CM)
PLANT HEIGHT: 4^1/$_2$ INCHES (11CM)
POT SIZE: 3–4 INCHES (8–10CM)

MILTONIOPSIS TWIN PEAKS

This American hybrid raised in 1991 has been widely acclaimed and has gained popularity for the delicate thread-like markings at the center of its lip. These, with the cherry-red areas of its pearl-white petals make a winning combination. The fragant flowers are large and well-shaped, with up to four blooms on a spike.

These are produced in early summer and will last for three weeks. The arching habit of the spikes keeps the flowers well clear of the foliage, which is not much taller. It grows best in intermediate temperatures. Keep moist all year round, but be careful not to overwater in winter.

FLOWER SIZE: 3^1/$_2$ INCHES (9CM) ACROSS
FLOWER SPIKE: 1 FOOT (30CM)
PLANT HEIGHT: 1 FOOT (30CM)
POT SIZE: 4 INCHES (10CM)

MILTONIOPSIS ANJOU 'SAINT PATRICK'

A good example of the flamboyant pansy orchid, the hybrid *M.* Anjou was raised in France in 1957 and remains a firm favorite today. This 'Saint Patrick' clone makes an ideal houseplant where intermediate temperatures can be provided for it, in a shady place well out of direct sun. The plant produces its flower spikes as the pseudobulbs mature, often making two spikes per pseudobulb. Each spike will bear two to four flowers, which should last about three weeks. During the summer flowering season, hybrids such as this one can be found in abundance in garden centers and other outlets. When buying, be sure to look for plump pseudobulbs.

FLOWER SIZE: 4 INCHES (10CM) ACROSS
FLOWER SPIKE: 1 FOOT (30CM)
PLANT HEIGHT: 9 INCHES (23CM)
POT SIZE: 5–6 INCHES (12–15CM)

MILTONIOPSIS RED TIDE

The lovely, vibrant pansy orchids are hard to beat when showing off their striking colors. The large, flat blooms are nearly always accompanied by a central decoration, often referred to as the "mask," and the yellow grooves are known as the "honey guide." This superb, fragrant hybrid is widely grown and is a popular color. It is a neat plant with pseudobulbs that will often produce two flower spikes any time in summer. The plant needs careful watering: allow it to dry out partially in between waterings and do not overwater. Keep it in the intermediate temperature range.

FLOWER SIZE: 3¹/₂ INCHES (9CM) ACROSS
FLOWER SPIKE: 1 FOOT (30CM)
PLANT HEIGHT: 1 FOOT (30CM)
POT SIZE: 4 INCHES (10CM)

MILTONIOPSIS
HERRALEXANDRE

This is a very fine modern hybrid, bred in the United States and registered in 1992. It combines the best of flower shape and color, and comes from a long line of similar, successful hybrids—its parents are *M*. Alexandre and *M*. Herrenhausen. Grow the plant in cool to intermediate temperatures in a shady position, and keep it moist. The fragrant blooms, which appear at any time during the spring and early summer, last for up to five weeks. During the fall months, a second flowering will often provide you with more blooms as a reminder of what is to come the following year. Each spike carries from one to three large, flat, pansy-shaped blooms.

FLOWER SIZE: 4 INCHES (10CM) ACROSS
FLOWER SPIKE: 1 FOOT (30CM)
PLANT HEIGHT: 10 INCHES (25CM)
POT SIZE: 4 INCHES (10CM)

MILTONIOPSIS ELIZABETH CASTLE

Raised in 1995 at the Eric Young Orchid Foundation in Jersey in the Channel Islands, home of the very best hybrids, this clone excels in its coloring and striking butterfly "mask." It has been bred from a long line of superb plants descended from the species *M. vexillaria*, found at high altitudes in the cloud forests of Colombia. This plant has retained the delicate fragrance of the species, which is most notable early in the day. It produces neat pseudobulbs and flowers in early summer and, often, again later in the year. The two to four large, flat blooms per spike will last for up to three weeks. Grow in intermediate temperatures and keep moist all year round, but be careful not to overwater in winter.

FLOWER SIZE: 4 INCHES (10CM) ACROSS
FLOWER SPIKE: 5–8 INCHES (12–20CM)
PLANT HEIGHT: 9 INCHES (23CM)
POT SIZE: 5–6 INCHES (12–15CM)

Dendrobium Ruby Beauty

This is a superb example of a hard-caned *Dendrobium* hybrid, of a type that is widely grown all over the world. Raised in 1990, these orchids are extremely tolerant and adaptable to various climates, but bear in mind that they are tropical plants and in their native environment, they make ideal garden plants. A mature plant will produce two to three flower spikes, each with about six or eight flowers, from the top portion of the elongated pseudobulbs during the fall. The pseudobulbs are leafed all along their length, and the leaves are retained during the winter, unlike in many dendrobiums which are deciduous. These hybrids are grown for the cut-flower trade in Singapore and Thailand and are exported far and wide. In flower shops and elsewhere they are known simply as Singapore orchids, and are sold in a multitude of colors just about everywhere in the world.

Flower size: $2^3/_4$ inches (7cm) across
Flower spike: 10 inches (25cm)
Plant height: 1 foot (30cm)
Pot size: 4 inches (10cm)

DENDROBIUM LONGICORNU

Discovered in India in 1830, this
dainty, small-growing species
produces slender canes leafed along
their whole length and covered with
small, dense, black-brown hairs.
The trumpet-shaped flowers, unusual
in the genus for their shape, do not
open fully and carry a spur at the
back where the sepals are fused.
The lip, like the rest of the flower, is
pure white, has deep orange-yellow
grooves along its length, and is
frilled at the edge. Several flowers
arise from the top portions of the
older canes and will last for three
weeks in mid- to late spring. The
plant needs a dry rest period in
winter but must not be allowed to
shrivel. During this time, check it
regularly and water occasionally
if necessary.

FLOWER SIZE: 2¹/₂ INCHES (6CM) LONG
PLANT HEIGHT: 10 INCHES (25CM)
POT SIZE: 3 INCHES (8CM)

EPIDENDRUM PARKINSONIANUM

This white-flowered species discovered in Mexico in 1887 produces heavy, spear-shaped leaves that hang down from diminutive, stem-like pseudobulbs. The spikes of one to two flowers last about three weeks and are produced from the base of the leaf where it joins the pseudobulb. This orchid looks best when grown on a slab of cork bark, where it will make copious aerial roots. It therefore requires a fairly cool aspect in which a humid atmosphere can be provided. Indoors, it can become difficult to keep the plant moist enough for it to progress and grow well. This lovely, summer-flowering species is fragrant at night, an indication that it is pollinated by night-flying moths.

FLOWER SIZE: 2$^{1}/_{2}$ INCHES (6CM) ACROSS
FLOWER SPIKE: 6 INCHES (15CM)
PLANT HEIGHT: 1 FOOT (30CM)
BARK SLAB: 1 FOOT (30CM) LONG

MASDEVALLIA MARY STAAL

New *Masdevallia* hybrids such as this outstanding clone bred in 1981 are becoming more readily available thanks to the extensive breeding program being carried out in the United States. This is creating a new generation of vigorous plants in a multitude of colors. White, however, is still the more unusual and this lovely variety has yellow-tipped tails to its broad sepals. The petals and lip are minute, and are hidden out of sight inside the tube formed by the sepals at the base of the flower. The plant does best in a cool environment where it needs shade for most of the year except during the shortest days. Keep it moist, but be careful not to overwater. The blooms are borne singly on the spike held well above the foliage and will last for two to three weeks in summer. A large plant with numerous flower spikes will flower much longer than this.

FLOWER SIZE: 1$^{1}/_{4}$ INCHES (3CM) ACROSS
FLOWER SPIKE: 10 INCHES (25CM)
PLANT HEIGHT: 6 INCHES (15CM)
POT SIZE: 3$^{1}/_{2}$ INCHES (9CM)

BULBOPHYLLUM ELASSICATUM

Belonging to the largest genus of
orchids, this pretty plant carries its
small, neat yellow flowers in a dense
raceme reminiscent of a fir cone. Its
pungent scent suggests pollination
by fruit flies. Its origins are
somewhat obscure, but it holds
a place among the smaller-growing,
small-flowered collectables and
is desirable for its relative ease of
growing. It produces small, rounded
pseudobulbs with a single leaf and
densely packed flowers that last two
to three weeks in early spring. This
orchid will grow in a small pot under
cool conditions, or it can be grown
on a piece of cork bark, which, if left
alone for many years, it will cover
with a solid ball of pseudobulbs
and leaves.

FLOWER SIZE: ¹/₂ INCH (1CM) ACROSS
PLANT HEIGHT: 6 INCHES (15CM)
POT SIZE: 4 INCHES (10CM)

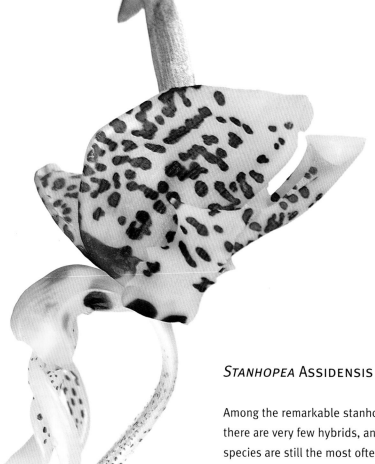

STANHOPEA ASSIDENSIS

Among the remarkable stanhopeas there are very few hybrids, and the species are still the most often grown. This is one of those rare hybrids, raised in Britain in 1922, and is a cross between two species, *S. wardii* and *S. tigrina*. Both parents originate from Central America, and the hybrid exhibits characteristics from each. It has the classical *Stanhopea* shape, the flowers being almost bat-like, with the lip and column held apart from the petals and sepals. The coloring is rich yellow overlaid with red spotting. When grown on into large plants, several flower spikes with up to six blooms per spike can be produced in one summer season, greatly extending the flowering period from a few days to several weeks. This orchid will suit most indoor temperatures but needs to be suspended in good light. Do not water when dormant. Like all stanhopeas, it must be grown in a hanging slatted basket to accommodate the flower spike that burrows through the potting mix to emerge underneath or at the side. Orchids are full of surprises!

FLOWER SIZE: 5 INCHES (12CM) LONG
FLOWER SPIKE: 4 INCHES (10CM)
PLANT HEIGHT: 1 FOOT (30CM)
BASKET SIZE: 6–8 INCHES (20–25CM)

STANHOPEA OCULATA

Of all the variants found among the orchids, one of the most curious genera is *Stanhopea*. This species, found in 1764 in Central and South America, is typical of the genus with its four to six huge, expressive blooms held underneath the plant on a vertical flower spike. The heavily spotted petals and sepals are drawn back to expose the waxy lip and column. At the base of the lip are two dark "eyes" which guide the pollinating insect. These extraordinary blooms will only last for three days, during which time they emit a strong perfume. The plant has pseudobulbs that produce a solitary, tough broad leaf; it also makes a strong root system. Like *Stanhopea* Assidensis (see opposite), this orchid will suit most indoor temperatures but needs to be grown in a slatted wooden basket suspended in good light.

FLOWER SIZE: 4 INCHES (10CM) ACROSS
FLOWER SPIKE: 6 INCHES (15CM)
PLANT HEIGHT: 1 FOOT (30CM)
BASKET SIZE: 6 INCHES (15CM)

BULBOPHYLLUM JERSEY

Within the huge genus *Bulbophyllum* are some of the weirdest of orchids. The species all come from the Old World and vary enormously in size and design. Jersey, raised on the island of the same name in the Channel Islands in 1996, is one of a very few hybrids, and it produces large, stunning flowers with a high gloss overlaying the intricately veined sepals. The small lip at the center of the bloom is typical of the genus and the petals are neatly folded back. The flowers are carried singly on drooping flower spikes throughout summer, and they will last for about three weeks. The plant produces rounded pseudobulbs with a single thick leaf. It is fairly easy to grow but be careful not to overwater in winter while it is at rest.

FLOWER SIZE: 7 INCHES (18CM) LONG
FLOWER SPIKE: 10 INCHES (25CM)
PLANT HEIGHT: 10 INCHES (25CM)
POT SIZE: 6 INCHES (15CM)

BURRAGEARA JUNGLE MOSS

This is a fancy new hybrid raised in 1991 within the *Oncidium* alliance, from which come so many fine and varied plants for indoor growing. It combines *Cochlioda*, *Miltonia*, *Odontoglossum,* and *Oncidium.* An exciting and colorful hybrid, it produces a tall, branching flower spike with a scattering of numerous flowers gaily patterned in red, yellow, and white. The plant is strong and robust, and has pseudobulbs similar to a true *Odontoglossum*. It needs to be grown cool and because of its complex breeding requires a bit more understanding than other hybrids within this alliance. Flowering time varies, but you can expect this plant to bloom for up to six weeks as the latest pseudobulb begins to mature and swell.

FLOWER SIZE: 2 INCHES (5CM) ACROSS
FLOWER SPIKE: 2 FEET (60CM)
PLANT HEIGHT: 1 FOOT (30CM)
POT SIZE: 5 INCHES (12CM)

NEEDS CARE

Finally, our "needs care" orchids are those that, in temperate climates, are most suited to growing in a greenhouse or conservatory, where better conditions can be created to suit their needs. Unlike in the home, where there is little flexibility in the provision of humidity or balanced light, in a greenhouse those aspects of culture can be more precisely controlled.

However, this does mean that these orchids will require more regular attention to maintain their good health and vigor. For instance, more time will be needed to ensure that the orchids' temperature, light, and humidity requirements are always in balance and never too extreme. An unattended greenhouse or conservatory can be a dangerous place for orchids: temperatures can soar out of control in just half an hour—something that does not happen within the home.

But if you have the time and experience to maintain a greenhouse and provide the right environment, you can expect the orchids to grow to their full potential. The rewards will lie in your enjoyment of their continuous healthy state and good flowering.

DENDROBIUM SIAM JEWEL

This is a warm-growing, hard-caned *Dendrobium* that, when given sufficient light, will produce sprays of pretty flowers from the top of the elongated pseudobulb throughout the spring. The blooms will last for a good four weeks. Various colors from white and pale pink, through mauve to dark purple have all been derived from species native to Australia. This exceptional hybrid from 1992 borders on the elusive blue. Extremely popular, it is grown worldwide for the pot-plant and cut-flower trade. However, an amateur can re-flower these orchids with the right conditions in a greenhouse: provide good light all year round and maximum temperatures in the warm range where possible. Keep the plants moist while they are growing, but allow them to dry out in winter.

FLOWER SIZE: 2 INCHES (5CM) ACROSS
FLOWER SPIKE: 10–15 INCHES (25–38CM)
PLANT HEIGHT: 8 INCHES (20CM)
POT SIZE: 5 INCHES (12CM)

VANDA ROBERT'S DELIGHT

This vibrantly colored hybrid comes from a long line of vandas bred from species native to India. These include the sky-blue *V. coerulea* and the cream, beige, and green *V. sanderiana* (syn. *Euanthe sanderiana*), both of which are rare in cultivation today. Their place has been taken in collections by the larger-flowered hybrids, which come in a wide range of exciting colors. The flowers are well rounded, with overlapping petals and sepals, and veined over their surface. The plants are fan-shaped, lack pseudobulbs, and produce their flower spikes from the leaf axils mainly during winter. This hybrid was raised in 1984 in Florida, where vandas grow best—they are easy to grow in all tropical areas. In temperate climates they are challenging and need extra care, but will reward you with flowers that last four to five weeks: all-year-round light, high temperatures, and humidity are essential for growth and flowering. In Southeast Asia these orchids are grown in their tens of thousands for the cut-flower trade.

FLOWER SIZE: 3¹/₂ INCHES (9CM) ACROSS
FLOWER SPIKE: 9 INCHES (23CM)
PLANT HEIGHT: 2 FEET (60CM)
BASKET SIZE: 4 INCHES (10CM)

VANDA BANGKOK PINK

Raised in Thailand in 1993, this robust and vigorous hybrid combines the best qualities that are sought in this type of orchid. Like most vandas, the plants will bloom at various times of the year, with six blooms to a spike and the flowers lasting for up to six weeks. When grown well, two flowerings can be expected in a year. The plants should be housed in slatted wooden baskets, where their extensive aerial roots can spread freely. This makes them unsuitable as houseplants, even in a warm room— they do best in tropical countries, where they are extremely easy. In temperate climates with colder winters these orchids are challenging to grow, although it can be done with care in a warm, humid greenhouse.

FLOWER SIZE: 4 INCHES (10CM) ACROSS
FLOWER SPIKE: 10 INCHES (25CM)
PLANT HEIGHT: 2 FEET (60CM)
BASKET SIZE: 4 INCHES (10CM)

DENDROBIUM EKAPOL

An attractive hybrid which burst onto the tropical cut-flower scene from Taiwan in 1982, this plant found favor both for floral decoration and the pot-plant trade. The combination of pink and white gives its blooms a fairy-tale appearance, with the added elegance of the East. The six to eight flowers that are borne in the fall on each spike will last for around four weeks. This plant and numerous others have all been derived from a very few species, the most dominant of which is *D. phalaenopsis* from Australia. It was first discovered on one of Captain Cook's expeditions and became known as the Cooktown orchid. Good all-year-round light is important for successful flowering and production of the season's growth, which is completed in a comparatively short time. The plant also needs a dry rest during the shortest days.

FLOWER SIZE: $2^{3}/_{4}$ INCHES (7CM) ACROSS
FLOWER SPIKE: 10 INCHES (25CM)
PLANT HEIGHT: 1 FOOT (30CM)
POT SIZE: 4 INCHES (10CM)

DENDROBIUM LLOYD STAINTON

Two of the hard-caned *Dendrobium* species—*D. superbiens* and *D. canaliculatum* from Australia—make up this worthwhile 1986 hybrid with its striking combination of white, red-lipped flowers. It is a tall-growing plant, leafed along the upper parts of its club-shaped pseudobulbs. The flower spikes arise from the top portion of the newly completed canes in late summer. The plant needs specialist care to address its fast, summer growing season, which is followed by a long resting period. All-year-round light is essential, with full sun in winter. Warm conditions suit it best.

FLOWER SIZE: 2 INCHES (5CM) ACROSS
FLOWER SPIKE: 1 FOOT (30CM)
PLANT HEIGHT: 2 FEET (60CM)
POT SIZE: 5 INCHES (12CM)

VASCOSTYLIS VIBOON VELVET X *ASCOCENDA* FIVE FRIENDSHIPS 'TWILIGHT'

This new and as yet unnamed hybrid combines *Vanda*, *Rhynchostylis*, and *Ascocentrum*. From this wide background one species, *R. coelestis*, is dominant, contributing to the size and shape of the flower, particularly its lip. This lovely orchid will flower for four to six weeks but is not a suitable subject for an indoor windowsill: in order to be grown well, it needs the sort of conditions— good light and humidity—that can only be given in a warm greenhouse. In the Northern Hemisphere it will flower mainly in spring and summer, while in the tropics, where its cultivation presents no problem, it flowers almost all year round.

FLOWER SIZE: 1 INCH (2.5CM) ACROSS
FLOWER SPIKE: 1 FOOT (30CM)
PLANT HEIGHT: 6 INCHES (15CM)
BASKET SIZE: 4 INCHES (10CM)

ASCOCENDA BICENTENNIAL

This multicolored hybrid from 1977 gets its vibrant hues from the species *Ascocentrum miniatum*. Through several generations of breeding it has influenced the coloring of this bigeneric cross, of which *Vanda* is the other genus parent. The dense, upright flower spike is another result of the *Ascocentrum* influence. The rich flowers are smaller than in *Vanda*, which is in keeping with the more compact plant. Twelve to fifteen flowers can be expected on a flower spike. These blooms are produced freely at various times of the year and will last about six weeks. Although this plant needs care when grown outside the tropics, it remains easier than the true vandas and can be grown and flowered in a warm greenhouse that enjoys good light all year round. Like all vandas and their allies, it is best grown suspended in a basket to allow its long aerial roots to hang freely.

FLOWER SIZE: 1¹/₂ INCHES (4CM) ACROSS
FLOWER SPIKE: 6 INCHES (15CM)
PLANT HEIGHT: 1 FOOT (30CM)
BASKET SIZE: 4 INCHES (10CM)

ONCIDIUM PUCK

This pretty and decorative 1978 hybrid belongs to a group known as the equitant oncidiums. They are all very distinctive in that they do not make pseudobulbs but have a number of spiky, hard leaves with masses of fine aerial roots. Given the right conditions, which include good light all year round, warmth, and being kept on the dry side, they will bloom almost continuously. The species originate from the West Indies; in the tropics, where they are extremely popular, they have been hybridized extensively, with the result that there is a whole range of colors from which to choose. The variation in markings is also almost limitless. As they are epiphytes, in tropical countries these orchids do extremely well when established on trees outdoors.

FLOWER SIZE: ³/₄ INCH (2CM) ACROSS
FLOWER SPIKE: 1 FOOT (30CM)
PLANT HEIGHT: 7 INCHES (18CM)
POT SIZE: 3 INCHES (8CM)

ADA AURANTIACA

This is a delightful species from Colombia, first introduced in 1854. With its vibrant orange, bell-shaped flowers closely set on an arching spike, this plant has long attracted the attention of the hybridizers. It is the species behind hybrid genera such as *Brassada* and others in the *Odontoglossum* alliance. While it imparts great vigor to its hybrid offspring, the species itself needs a little more care to ensure that it does not suffer from rot, which can plague new growths if conditions become too wet or cold during the winter months. Grow it cool alongside other odontoglossums, and keep it on the dry side during winter. Up to twelve tubular flowers per spike appear in spring and last for up to three weeks.

FLOWER SIZE: 1 INCH (2.5CM) ACROSS
FLOWER SPIKE: 10 INCHES (25CM)
PLANT HEIGHT: 10 INCHES (25CM)
POT SIZE: 4 INCHES (10CM)

Cultivating orchids

In the following pages we set out the basic requirements needed for sound orchid culture. Orchids are extremely tolerant plants and will adapt to a whole range of conditions if they have to. Provided their basic needs are met, they will thrive for many years, growing and flowering in their seasons to give immense pleasure.

If you cannot give the orchids exactly the right temperatures or amounts of light recommended here, try to get as close as possible. If a particular plant does not appear to be doing well in one position, move it to another until you find the place where it responds best. However, remember that orchids are slow growing and are therefore slow to react to changes in their living conditions. It would be a mistake, for instance, to move a plant too frequently without giving it a chance to settle down. It may take several months, or a whole growing season, before you can determine whether a plant has done better or worse in a certain situation.

The proof of this would be whether or not the latest pseudobulb is at least equal in size to the previous one. New pseudobulbs or, in the case of phalaenopsis, new leaves, that are smaller than previously, are an indication that the plant has not done well, so it may be time to move it elsewhere.

Paphiopedilums do well as houseplants, enjoying warm conditions away from bright sun. Keep them evenly watered throughout the year, but avoid saturation. This can occur when using a decorative container that does not provide proper drainage.

TEMPERATURE

In general, orchids tolerate a wide range of temperatures, from a minimum of 50°F (10°C) to a maximum of 90°F (32°C). The cool-growing orchids, which include cymbidiums, odontoglossums, and many more, require a minimum winter night temperature of 50°F (10°C), rising during the day to at least 60°F (16°C). Intermediate orchids, which include miltoniopsis and cattleyas, plus allies of cattleyas as well as some dendrobiums, require a little more warmth—55°F (13°C) on winter nights and at least 65°F (19°C) during the day. Most of these can be accommodated in a temperate climate in a home with a heating system.

Warm-growing orchids need 60–65°F (16–18°C) on winter nights, rising as much as possible during the day. In all but the tropics these orchids grow best in a conservatory or greenhouse where these temperatures can be maintained by artificial heating. An exception is phalaenopsis, which are happy as houseplants in a warm room.

AS HOUSEPLANTS

Our "easy" and "fairly easy" orchids (see pages 20–105) are usually at home indoors, while the smaller types, such as miltoniopsis and odontoglossums, will grow on a

All orchids require shading from direct sunlight. This is particularly true for miltoniopsis, whose soft foliage can easily be burnt. Place shades, curtains, or greenhouse netting between the glass and your orchids during summer.

windowsill. In the Northern Hemisphere, during summer, a north-facing aspect is ideal. This gives adequate light but not direct sunlight, which can burn the foliage. You can use other aspects provided the window has a shade or net curtains to create shade. In winter, place the orchids in a more southerly aspect, where the lower position of the sun will not harm them.

Stand the orchid pots in a humidity tray on a layer of expanded clay pellets covered with water so that the orchids are not standing directly in the wet, but just above it. Grow other small, slow-growing houseplants alongside. This not only looks attractive but provides extra humidity.

In summer, place larger orchids, like cymbidiums, in a cool, shady position outdoors on a bench or upturned pot to protect them from slugs, snails, wood lice, and worms. This will provide them with better light, which is often hard to achieve indoors for orchids that are too large for a windowsill.

IN A CONSERVATORY OR GREENHOUSE

Our "needs care" orchids (see pages 106–117) must be housed in a conservatory or greenhouse. Here you can create more precise conditions and grow a much wider range of orchids. One essential for conservatory or greenhouse culture is a maximum/minimum thermometer to record daytime maximum and nighttime minimum temperatures. This helps you decide if you need to adjust the heating or ventilation. Orchids that are overheated in summer or too cold in winter will become stressed and will stop growing.

In summer, the temperature required by warm-growing orchids can be achieved easily without any extra heating, but ventilation and shading may be necessary (see below). In winter you will need heating either from a gas- or oil-fired boiler, with hot water pipes or radiators under the benches, or, in a small greenhouse, by using an electric fan heater.

Ventilation

Orchids thrive on fresh air, and good ventilation is essential throughout the year. During the winter months, provide as much fresh air as possible without causing a sudden drop in temperature. Do this by opening the ventilator just a crack whenever possible.

Most greenhouses incorporate ridge ventilators, with smaller ventilators at ground level. The temperature can rise extremely quickly on a hot day, and it is essential that

To provide humidity, place the orchids on a humidity tray or saucer with pebbles in the base. Stand the plant on top of the pebbles, which can be kept wet. Take care not to immerse the pot in pebbles, as this would keep the plant too wet.

Blinds provide an ideal form of shading for your orchids, both indoors and in the greenhouse. On dull, sunless days, they can be raised to give the plants maximum light, and on bright days lowered to provide protection from the sun.

the ventilators open early, well before the temperature climbs too high. Temperature-controlled ventilators are best, as they open and close automatically.

For additional air movement, you could install a thermostatically controlled extractor fan at the apex at one end of the greenhouse and louvres at ground level at the opposite end, or you could run a small circulating fan day and night.

Shading

In their natural habitat some orchids can stand a great deal of direct sunlight but under glass they will easily scorch, overheat, and be damaged irreparably. It is essential, therefore, that the conservatory or greenhouse is shaded from the earliest spring months onward to protect young growths and buds.

Many types of shading are available. For a greenhouse the most popular is netting, which is most effective when placed on the outside. The best has an aluminum strip woven into the material to reflect heat and so keep the greenhouse cool. For those awkward corners by the apex, it may be easier to use greenhouse paint shading, applied in spring and removed in the fall.

Some orchid houses are supplied complete with shades, which can be controlled automatically by light-sensitive switches. In a conservatory, where looks are important, shades are most suitable, but some paint shading may also be necessary.

Humidity

Humidity is essential for orchids but is continually lost through the ventilators, so you need to keep it replenished. The simplest way of doing this is either to have an earth floor that you damp down daily, or benches to stand the orchids on, with staging below.

The easiest benches to maintain are made from open, slatted wood strips. The staging beneath can consist of large plastic trays covered with capillary matting. When the plants above are watered, the matting retains the run-off.

You can provide extra humidity with an automatic sprinkler system below the bench. Another sprinkler rail can be placed above the plants to mist the foliage, but avoid spraying flowers or buds as this may cause spotting. Alternatively, you can install a humidifier.

When watering, use a watering can with a spout and water directly onto the surface of the potting mix, flooding the whole pot in one application. You can repeat this if the potting mix was very dry at the outset. Add feed to the water at about every third watering.

CULTIVATION

Most orchids in cultivation are epiphytes. These will not grow in a soil-based potting mix but need an open, free-draining material. The traditional growing medium for orchids is made from pine-bark chippings, with various modifications in the different countries where orchids are grown. Today, in the major countries of mass production, orchids are raised in horticultural rock wool, an inorganic man-made fiber originally developed for insulation. It is good for growing orchids because it does not rot and the roots can penetrate it easily.

Various orchid potting mixes are available through specialist orchid nurseries and some garden centers. If you are in any doubt as to which type of potting mix to use, discuss this with the seller when you purchase your plants. Whichever medium is used, do not mix two types together: bark and horticultural rock wool are not compatible and require different watering and feeding regimes.

Orchid potting medium can consist of varying sizes of organic bark chippings (center, left, and rear), or inorganic, artificial horticultural foam sponge mixed with dried sphagnum moss (front). Another alternative is horticultural rock wool (not shown).

Watering

Orchids like to be moist while they are growing and on the dry side when dormant. Most rest during the winter and they often bloom then. While some orchids, such as cymbidiums, the *Odontoglossum* alliance, phalaenopsis, and paphiopedilums, have only a short resting period and must therefore be kept moist throughout the year, others are dormant for several weeks or months. It is these, which include the coelogynes, encyclias, and dendrobiums, that must be kept drier. This means giving no more than an occasional watering if the pseudobulbs begin to shrivel. As soon as the new growth is seen in early spring, normal watering can be resumed.

For normal watering, give the orchids a good drenching, flooding the surface of the potting mix and if necessary repeating so there is plenty of water running through the pot. Most of it will quickly drain out, leaving the potting mix moist but not saturated. Water again only when the plant begins to dry out, but before it becomes completely dry. Plants growing in rock wool should never be allowed to get too dry, except in winter.

The larger the surface of the potting mix, the easier it is to water. A plant that has filled its pot with roots and is in need of repotting will need more water than a newly repotted plant with plenty of room. If necessary, dunk a root-filled pot in water and allow it to soak for about half an hour. In summer, most orchids should also be lightly sprayed over their leaves each day to keep them fresh.

Cymbidiums will often push themselves out of their pots by their roots (far left). This tells you that they need to go into a larger pot. Trim off any dead roots (left) before repotting into a pot 2 inches (5cm) larger.

Use a small measuring jug to measure out the correct amount of fertilizer granules and water for your orchids. This will avoid any danger of overfeeding with too strong a dose of feed, which could burn the roots.

Feeding

Special nitrogen- or phosphate-based orchid feeds are available in granule or liquid form. According to the season, apply nitrates for growth or phosphates for flowers. Always follow the manufacturer's instructions carefully. Alternatively, use a standard houseplant feed diluted to half-strength.

Orchids growing in horticultural rock wool or other inorganic materials need more feeding while those in a bark or other organic mix receive most of the nutrients they require as the potting mix breaks down. Generally speaking though, apply feed at every third watering in winter, increasing to every other watering during spring and early summer. By late summer, as growths are maturing, reduce feeding to once every third watering.

It is possible to overfeed orchids, which may burn the roots. If in doubt, reduce the feed, and apply it only to healthy plants. Any orchid that has lost its roots should not be given feed until new roots have grown.

Repotting

Orchids require regular repotting, roughly every other year, or when the plant has filled its pot with roots and there is no room for further growth. Repot in spring, using an appropriate potting mix. The ideal time is when you can see the new growth starting.

Remove the plant from its pot and tease out the old potting mix from between the roots. Discard any dead roots—these are soft and often blackened, and the outer covering can be pulled away, leaving an inner wire-like core—by cutting them back to the base of the plant. Live roots are white and fleshy. If these are very long, trim back to about 6 inches (15cm). Place the plant in a pot about 2 inches (5cm) larger than the previous one, and compact firmly with potting mix so the plant is well supported. The base of the pseudobulbs or new growths must be level with the surface of the potting mix, not buried in it. Allow the plant to settle for a day or two before giving it a good watering.

Propagation

Large orchids with many pseudobulbs can be divided by cutting between the pseudobulbs. You can make two or more plants from one, but leave at least four good pseudobulbs and a new growth on each division. If the pieces are too small, they will not flower. Paphiopedilums and phragmipediums do not make pseudobulbs but can be divided in a similar way. Monopodial orchids such as phalaenopsis cannot readily be propagated by this method.

You can divide your orchids to prevent them from becoming too large. Leave at least four pseudobulbs on each division by cutting between the rhizome with a sharp knife.

TROUBLESHOOTING

Orchids can suffer from various ailments, most of which are related to cultivation.

Overwatering

Most evergreen orchids, which include all those featured in this book, will occasionally, in the normal course of things, drop a few of their oldest leaves from the back of the plant. Premature or rapid loss of a lot of foliage, on the other hand, can mean overwatering, and if the plant has lost its roots, too, this is confirmed.

When this happens, remove the plant from its pot, discard all the old potting mix, trim back the dead roots, and remove old pseudobulbs that have lost their leaves. This will reduce the size of the plant, and the leading part—the part that bears the new growths—can be potted up. With care, more new growth will start from the base, followed by new roots, but it can be several years before the plant will bloom again.

Underwatering

Underwatering will cause shriveling of the pseudobulbs and limp foliage. A good soak in a pail of water will usually be sufficient to plump up the pseudobulbs once again.

Discolored foliage

Yellowing of the foliage can be a sign of too much light, in which case provide more shade or move the plant. Alternatively, it may indicate a lack of food. Lightly spray the leaves with a foliar feed regularly until they regain their mid-green color.

Older leaves may develop black tips in winter and this is usually a sign of temperatures that are too low, or a combination of cold and wet. Trim the tips back and increase the heating slightly.

Bold black streaking along the length of the leaves may be a sign of virus disease. This can appear if growing conditions are poor. There is no cure, but improved cultivation may slow its progress. Virus can spread to other orchids, so keep any suspect plants in isolation or discard them altogether.

Pests

Check your orchids regularly for signs of insect pests. Mealybugs, which are small, pinkish in color and covered in a woolly substance, scale insects, which are hard and scaly, and red spider mites, which are almost too small to be seen but show up on the undersides of leaves as silvery patches, can all attack orchids. All three can be treated using a small paintbrush dipped in industrial alcohol.

INDEX

SOURCES AND SUPPLIERS

For the largest orchid society in the world visit the American Orchid Society at www.orchidweb.org

For a database of orchid growers, societies, and related orchid sites in the United States and countries around the world, go to www.orchidlink.com

For magazines, books and periodicals on orchids, go to www.orchidweb.org/publications.html www.orchidmall.com/reading.htm